Fiat 128 1969-79 Autobook

By the Autobooks Team of Writers and Illustrators

Fiat 128 1969-79
Fiat 128 Special 1974-76
Fiat 128 C, CL 1976-79
Fiat 128 Rally 1972-76
Fiat 128 SL 1972-75
Fiat 128 3P Berlinetta 1976-79

Autobooks Ltd. Golden Lane Brighton BN1 2QJ England

The AUTOBOOK series of Workshop Manuals is the largest in the world and covers the majority of British and Continental motor cars, as well as the majority of Japanese and Australian models.

Whilst every care has been taken to ensure correctness of information it is obviously not possible to guarantee complete freedom from errors or omissions or to accept liability arising from such errors or omissions.

CONTENTS

Acknowledgement

Introduction

ISBN 0 85147 896 4

First Edition   1972
Reprinted   1973
Second Edition, fully revised   1973
Third Edition, fully revised   1974
Fourth Edition, fully revised   1975
Fifth Edition, fully revised   1977
Sixth Edition, fully revised   1978
Seventh Edition, fully revised   1979

725

Printed in Brighton England for Autobooks Ltd by G. Beard and Son Ltd
Bound in Hove England for Autobooks Ltd by Jilks Ltd   F

INTRODUCTION

This do-it-yourself Workshop Manual has been specially written for the owner who wishes to maintain his vehicle in first class condition and to carry out the bulk of his own servicing and repairs. Considerable savings on garage charges can be made, and one can drive in safety and confidence knowing the work has been done properly.

Comprehensive step-by-step instructions and illustrations are given on most dismantling, overhauling and assembling operations. Certain assemblies require the use of expensive special tools, the purchase of which would be unjustified. In these cases information is included but the reader is recommended to hand the unit to the agent for attention.

Throughout the Manual hints and tips are included which will be found invaluable, and there is an easy to follow fault diagnosis at the end of each chapter.

Whilst every care has been taken to ensure correctness of information it is obviously not possible to guarantee complete freedom from errors or omissions or to accept liability arising from such errors or omissions.

Instructions may refer to the righthand or lefthand sides of the vehicle or the components. These are the same as the righthand or lefthand of an observer standing behind the vehicle and looking forward.

Warren Ball with his Fiat 128 3P Berlinetta

CHAPTER 1

THE ENGINE

1:1 Description

Although two sizes of engine are fitted to the cars covered by this manual, they differ only in certain dimensional specifications which are given in full in **Technical Data** at the end of the book, and one set of instructions will be adequate for servicing both sizes. It is an in-line four-cylinder unit, transversally mounted and inclined forward by 20 deg. in the engine compartment. A single overhead camshaft is provided, driven by synthetic rubber toothed belt with steel cable reinforcement, drive being taken from the crankshaft. This belt also drives the engine auxiliary shaft which operates the distributor, oil pump and fuel pump. Sectional views of the engine assembly are shown in **FIGS 1:1** and **1:2**.

The spheroidal cast iron cylinder block is integral with the crankcase. The split-type cylinder head is of light alloy and consists of a bottom section fixed to the cylinder block, which carries the valves, valve springs and sparking plugs and a top section fixed to the bottom section, which carries the camshaft The camshaft is supported in five plain bearings.

The spheroidal cast steel crankshaft has integral balance weights and is provided with five plain shell bearings, all of which are pressure lubricated. Axial thrust is accommodated by the main bearing nearest to the flywheel.

The light alloy pistons are of the auto-thermal type, having integrally cast steel retaining rings and full skirts.

Two compression rings and one oil control ring are fitted to each piston. Gudgeon pins on the 1116 cc engines are a free fit in the pistons and shrunk-fitted into the connecting rod small ends.

Engines of 1290 cc capacity have a small end bush which is pressed in, the gudgeon pins are retained by circlips.

The gear type oil pump, driven by the engine auxiliary shaft. is located in the lower part of the crankcase. Pressure oil is fully filtered before being passed to the lubrication points in the engine. The external oil filter is of the fullflow type and incorporates a relief valve which operates to return excess oil to the sump in the event of oil pressure rising higher than the safe maximum.

1:2 Removing the engine

The normal operations of decarbonizing and servicing the cylinder head, camshaft and valve servicing and such operations as the renewal of the camshaft drive belt can be carried out without removing the engine. A major overhaul, however, can only be carried out with the engine removed from the car. If the operator is not a skilled automobile engineer, it is suggested that he will find much useful information in **Hints on Maintenance and Overhaul** at the end of this manual and that he read it before starting work. The method of engine removal

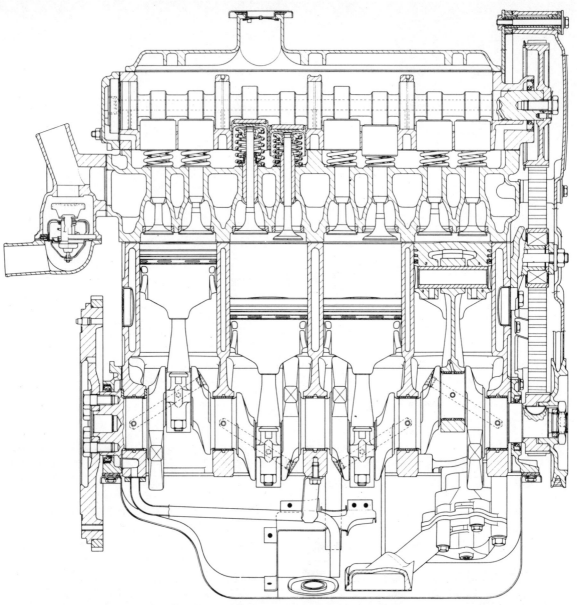

FIG 1:1   Longitudinal section through the engine

which follows describes the removal of the engine and gearbox as an assembly, it not being advisable to attempt removal of the engine alone. It must be stressed that the lifting equipment used to remove the assembly from the car should be sound, firmly based and not likely to collapse under the weight it will be supporting.

Removal:

1 Raise the car on stands or other suitable supports to give room for under-car engine removal. Raise the bonnet, remove the spare wheel and disconnect the battery. Take off the lower guards.

2 Drain the engine cooling system as described in **Chapter 4,** collecting the coolant in a clean container if it contains antifreeze which is to be re-used.

3 Remove the air filter and disconnect the accelerator and choke controls from the carburetter. Disconnect the fuel feed pipe. Disconnect the engine steady, and the exhaust pipe from the manifold.

4 Disconnect the water hoses from the radiator, water pump and heater system.

5 Remove the distributor cap. Disconnect the wires between the coil and the distributor. Disconnect all electrical connections between the engine and the

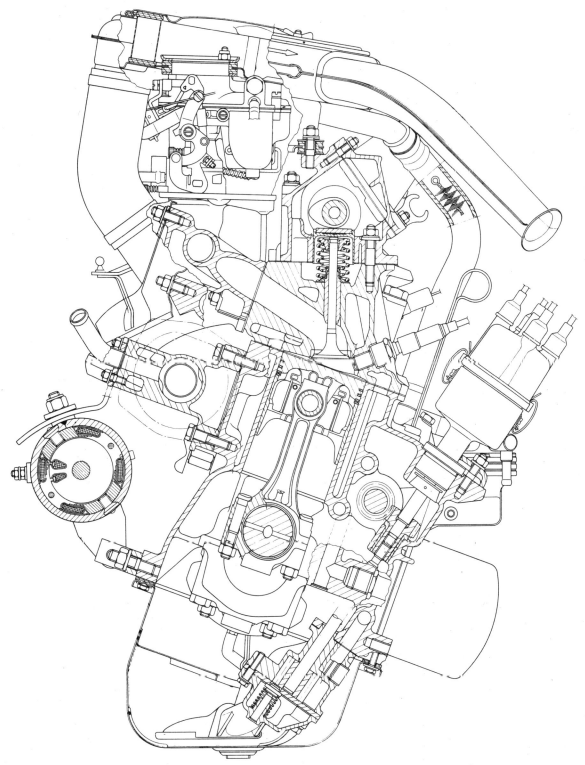

FIG 1:2   Transverse section through the engine

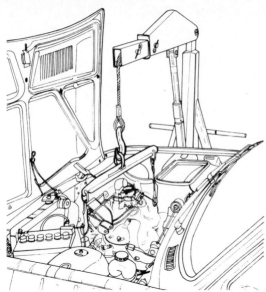

FIG 1:3 Removing the engine and gearbox assembly

car frame, including the wires to the oil pressure and temperature sender units.

6 Remove the anti-roll bar as described in **Chapter 7.** Remove the exhaust pipe support bracket from the transmission housing, and also the earthing lead.

7 Attach the lifting equipment to the engine lifting lugs as shown in **FIG 1:3.** Take the weight of the engine, then remove the right and left side silentbloc supports and the tie rods.

8 Disconnect the clutch control as described in **Chapter 5.** Disconnect the transmission units as described in **Chapter 6.** Detach the gearchange control rod and the speedometer cable from the gearbox.

9 Remove the centre crossmember from beneath the gearbox, then lower the engine and gearbox assembly from the engine compartment, working the transmission shafts out of the struts and tying them to

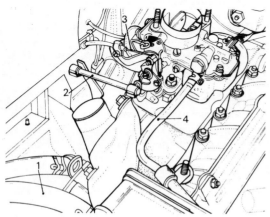

FIG 1:4 Items to be disconnected before cylinder head removal

prevent withdrawal from their differential ends, and transfer the assembly to an engine stand or bench.

Refitting:

Refitting the engine and gearbox assembly is a reversal of the removal procedure. New hoses must be obtained to replace any which show signs of deterioration and the required quantities of engine and gearbox oil obtained. When installation is complete, rock the engine on its mountings to settle them, then tighten the mountings securely. Do this before refitting the ancilliary components to avoid mounting stresses, particularly in the exhaust system.

On completion, check the valve clearances as described in **Section 1:8** and the ignition timing as as described in **Chapter 3.** If necessary, adjust the carburetter as described in **Chapter 2.**

1:3 Removing and refitting the head

Removal:

Make sure that the engine has cooled completely before starting work. Disconnect the battery and detach the cable from the cylinder head support. Drain the cooling system as described in **Chapter 4,** collecting the coolant in a clean container if it contains antifreeze which is to be re-used. Remove the air filter.

Refer to **FIG 1:4** and disconnect the heater hose 1, the accelerator control 2, the choke cable 3 and the fuel feed pipe 4. Refer to **FIG 1:5** and disconnect the hoses 1, 2 and 3, the carburetter heating hose 4, the engine steady 5 and the exhaust pipe to manifold connection 6.

Disconnect the crankcase breather hose. Detach the sparking plug leads from the sparking plugs, then remove the sparking plugs. Disconnect the temperature sender wire.

Undo the fixing screws and remove the plastic timing gear cover, as shown in **FIG 1:6.** Remove the sheet metal belt protector from the cylinder block and cylinder head. **FIG 1:7** shows the timing belt and pulleys. Release the timing belt tensioner shown in **FIG 1:8,** release the belt tension as described in **Section 1:6** and remove the belt from the camshaft pulley.

Unlock and remove the nuts, screws and washers holding the cylinder head in position, special spanners 50131/1 and 50131/2 being the correct tools for this operation. Remove the toothed belt protective cover fixing screw, this screw being located below the intermediate shaft pulley. Remove the cylinder head and gasket.

Refitting:

Turn the engine until the timing marks on the flywheel and on the pulleys are correctly aligned, as described in **Section 1:7.** Clean off all traces of old gasket material from the head and cylinder block, taking care not to damage the joint face of the light alloy cylinder head. With the mating surfaces clean and dry, place a new head gasket in position, making sure that the word 'ALTO' is facing upwards, and refit head, first making sure that the camshaft pulley is still correctly aligned, inserting the head attaching screws and nuts finger tight. Tighten the attaching screws and nuts in the order shown in **FIG 1:9** in two stages; first to 29 lb ft and then to the specified torque of 69.0 lb ft. Refit the remaining parts in

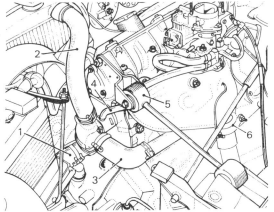

FIG 1:5 Items to be disconnected before cylinder head removal

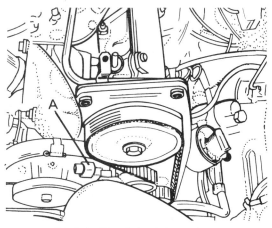

FIG 1:8 The timing belt tensioner

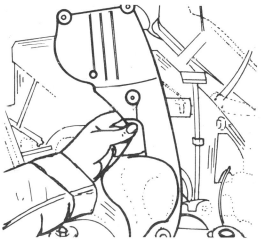

FIG 1:6 Removing the plastic timing gear cover

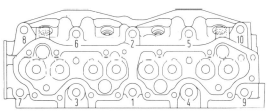

FIG 1:9 Tightening sequence for cylinder head screws and nuts

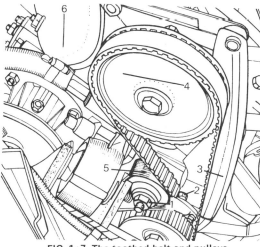

FIG 1:7 The toothed belt and pulleys

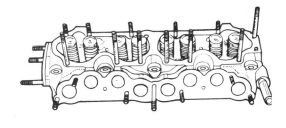

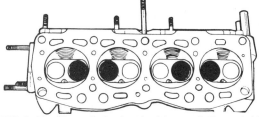

FIG 1:10 The cylinder head with camshaft assembly removed

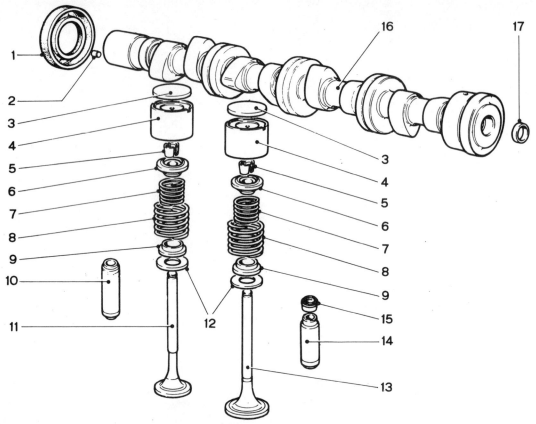

FIG 1 :11   The camshaft and valve gear

Key to Fig 1 :11   1 Seal   2 Pin   3 Adjusting capsule   4 Tappet   5 Cotters   6 Valve spring seat   7 Inner valve spring
8 Outer valve spring   9 Valve spring seat   10 Valve guide   11 Exhaust valve   12 Washers   13 Inlet valve   14 Valve guide
15 Seal   16 Camshaft   17 Bush

the reverse order of removal, checking the belt tension as described in **Section 1 : 6**, the valve timing as described in **Section 1 : 7** and the ignition timing as described in **Chapter 3**.

1 : 4 Servicing the head and valves

Dismantling :

Remove the thermostat housing complete with thermostat. Remove the toothed belt protecting cover. Remove the camshaft cover and gasket, then remove the top section of the cylinder head complete with camshaft. Take care not to lose the centring dowels during this operation. **FIG 1 : 10** shows the cylinder head assembly with the camshaft unit removed.

Remove the tappets with their adjusting capsules, keeping each capsule with the correct tappet and keeping both parts in the correct order for refitting in their original positions. Remove the steel screen assembly complete with the inlet and exhaust manifolds.

Use a suitable valve spring compressor to remove the valve gear from the cylinder head. With the spring compressed, remove the split taper collets then remove the compressor tool and collect the valve, springs, spring

seats and washers. The valve gear components are shown in **FIG 1 :11**. Keep all valve gear components in the correct order for refitting in their original positions.

Valves :

When the valves have been cleaned of carbon deposits they must be inspected for serviceability. Valves with bent stems or badly burned heads must be renewed. Valves that are pitted can be recut at a service station, but if they are too far gone for this remedial treatment, new valves will be required. The correct valve seat angles are shown in **FIG 1 :12**.

Valve guides :

Valve guides that are worn or scored must be renewed. As the guides must be pressed into or out of place, reamed, then the valve seat recut for concentricity, this work should be carried out by a service station having the necessary special equipment.

Valve seat inserts :

Valve seat inserts that are pitted or burned must be refaced or, if they are too far gone for remedial treatment,

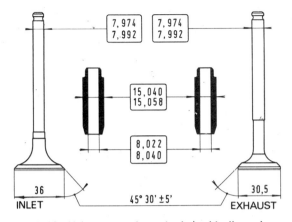

FIG 1:12 Valve seat angles and valve guide dimensions

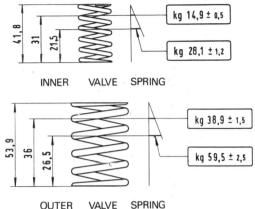

INNER VALVE SPRING

OUTER VALVE SPRING

FIG 1:14 Valve spring test measurements

renewed. As either operation requires the use of special equipment, this work should be carried out by a service station. The correct angles for valve seat angles at the cylinder head inserts are shown in **FIG 1:13**.

Valve springs:

Test the valve springs by comparison with the figures in **FIG 1:14** by loading each spring the stated amount and checking that the compressed length is not less than the figure given. Alternatively, compare the efficiency of the old springs against that of new units. To do this, insert both the old and new springs end to end with a metal plate between them into the jaws of a vice. If the old spring is weakened, it will close up first when pressure is applied. Take care that the springs do not fly out of the vice under pressure. Any spring which is shorter or weaker than standard should be renewed.

Decarbonizing and valve reseating:

Avoid the use of sharp tools which could damage the light alloy cylinder head surfaces. Remove all traces of carbon deposits from the combustion chambers, inlet and exhaust ports and joint faces. Plug the waterways and oil holes in the top surface of the cylinder block with pieces of rag to prevent the entry of dirt, then clean the carbon from the piston crowns.

The manufacturers do not recommend grinding in the valves to their seats using carborundum paste in the conventional manner. They specify the use of specialized equipment for re-facing the valves and valve seats, which makes this an operation which should be entrusted to the service station where the correct tools will be available. A special gauge will also be necessary to check that the valve stem height above the cylinder head is correct when the re-facing is completed.

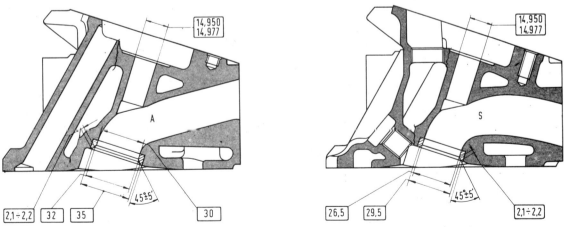

FIG 1:13 Valve seat insert angles for inlet valves (left), exhaust valves (right)

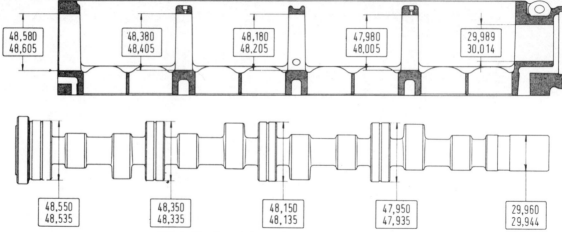

FIG 1:15 Camshaft bearing and journal dimensions

Reassembly:

This is a reversal of the removal procedure. Use engine oil to lubricate the moving parts during reassembly, particularly the valve stems and the camshaft lobes. Make sure that all valve gear parts are refitted in their original positions, unless they have been renewed. On completion, check the valve clearances and adjust if necessary, as described in **Section 1:8**.

1:5 Camshaft removal and refitting

Removal:

Remove the air filter, then remove the camshaft cover from the top of the cylinder head. Turn the engine until the timing marks are in line as in **FIG 1:16**. Remove the timing belt as described in **Section 1:6**. Remove the top section of the cylinder head complete with the camshaft.

Bend back the locking plate and release the toothed pulley retaining nut. Remove the toothed pulley. Remove the rear camshaft cover and gasket, then remove the camshaft from the side opposite the pulley.

Examine the cams and bearing surfaces for wear or damage. The camshaft should be renewed if excessive wear or scoring is evident, or if the shaft is out of true. **FIG 1:15** shows the dimensions in millimetres for the camshaft bearings and journals. Note that, due to the need for special equipment, the renewal of camshaft bearings should be carried out by a service station.

Refitting:

Place the camshaft into the top section of the cylinder head and refit the seal on the toothed pulley side. Refit the rear camshaft cover, using a new gasket. Refit the toothed pulley and lock the nut with the locking plate. Refit the top section of the cylinder head after turning the camshaft so that its timing mark is correctly aligned using a new gasket. Refit the toothed belt as described in **Section 1:6**. Replace the camshaft cover and the air filter.

1:6 Timing belt renewal

This operation can be performed with the engine still mounted in the car, but the operator must be prepared for a certain amount of inconvenience of access and the removal of certain other components, e.g. the generator drive.

Before removing the timing belt, either turn the engine so that the timing marks shown in **FIG 1:16** are in alignment or mark the position of all three pulleys to ensure correct refitment of the belt. DO NOT turn either pulley once the belt is removed or the timing will be lost and internal damage caused to valves and pistons.

Remove the plastic cover over the timing gear and release the belt tensioner shown in **FIG 1:16** by placing a wrench on the pulley nut 4 and pressing in an anti-clockwise direction until the tensioner body 12 depresses the spring and piston 13 as far as possible and remove the belt from the pulleys.

Ensure that all timing marks are correctly set and fit the new belt, carefully avoiding any acute angles which might damage the internal construction of the belt. Lock the tensioner in position by tightening the pulley nut 4 to 32.5 lb ft and re-check the timing marks before fitting the plastic cover.

Check the ignition timing as detailed in **Section 3:5, Chapter 3** if necessary.

1:7 Valve timing

Provided that the instructions given above in **Section 1:6** are followed, valve timing will be necessary only when the camshaft has been disturbed for any reason. Since it is possible that the valves will foul the pistons if either the camshaft or crankshaft is rotated with the belt removed, it is essential that the camshaft should be lifted clear of the valves before turning the crankshaft or the camshaft into the correct timing position shown in the illustration.

Check that No. 1 piston is at TDC and the crankshaft pulley mark 7 in line with the fixed timing mark 5. Check —rotate the shaft 8 if necessary—that the rotor in the distributor is pointing to the segment in the distributor cap for No. 1 sparking plug. Set the camshaft pulley 1 with the timing marks 2 and 3 in line as shown and then tighten down the camshaft housing assembly, making sure that the timing marks are still in alignment.

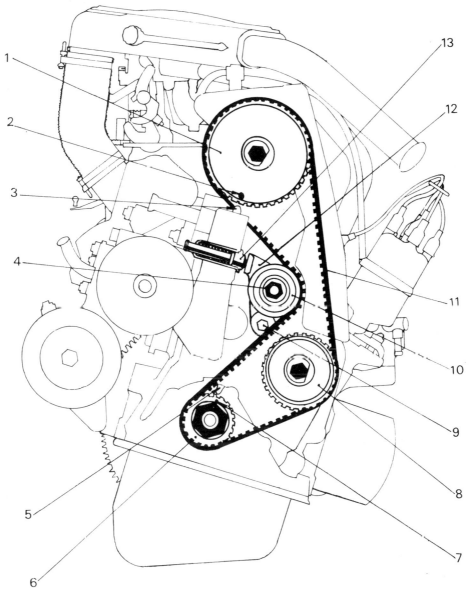

FIG 1:16   The toothed belt, pulleys and timing marks

Key to Fig 1:16   1 Camshaft pulley   2 Timing mark   3 Fixed timing mark   4 Tensioner nut   5 Fixed timing mark
6 Crankshaft pulley   7 Timing mark   8 Auxiliary shaft pulley   9 Tensioner pivot   10 Tensioner pulley   11 Toothed belt
12 Tensioner body   13 Tensioner spring and piston

If the cylinder head is being refitted after servicing, make sure that the camshaft pulley is correctly located before installation.

With all timing marks correctly aligned, fit the toothed belt and set the tensioner. Recheck the alignment. The engine valve timing will now be correctly set, but the ignition timing must be reset as described in **Chapter 3** as no reference marks are used for accurate alignment of the auxiliary shaft pulley. Check the valve clearances as described next.

1:8 Valve clearance adjustment

The correct adjustment of valve clearance is important as it affects engine timing and performance considerably. Excessive clearance will reduce valve lift and opening duration and reduce engine performance, causing excessive wear on the valve gear components and noisy operation. Insufficient or zero clearance will again affect engine timing and, in some circumstances, can hold the valve clear of its seat. This will result in much reduced performance and the possibility of burned valves and

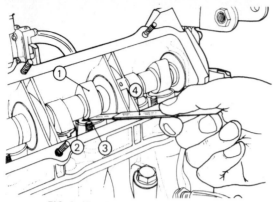

FIG 1:17 Checking valve clearances

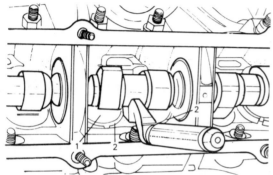

FIG 1:18 Locking the tappet in the fully depressed position

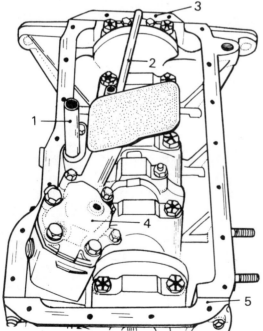

FIG 1:19 The oil pump and return pipes

seats. Valve clearances should be checked every 10,000 kilometres as routine maintenance and, additionally, whenever the cylinder head has been serviced. Checking should also be carried out at any time when valve gear noise is noticed.

The valve clearances must be checked and adjusted when the engine is cold, so allow it to cool down completely before proceeding. The correct clearances are as follows:

1116 cc engines	inlet .40 mm, exhaust .50 mm
1290 cc engines	inlet .40 mm, exhaust .50 mm

Remove the air cleaner and the camshaft cover. Turn the engine as described in **Section 1:7**, so that the cam lobe over the valve being checked is vertically positioned as shown in **FIG 1:17**. Check the clearance between the cam and the adjusting capsule, using feeler gauges. Work in this manner until all valves have been checked, noting the clearance readings for the valves as they are taken. If any clearance is incorrect, adjustment must be carried out in the following manner.

Turn the engine until the cam lobe above the valve in question is vertical. Position special tool A60421 bearing on both the inlet and exhaust tappets, turn the handle of the tool to lock the tappet in the fully depressed position, as shown in **FIG 1:18**. Use tool A.87001 or compressed air to eject the adjusting capsule from the tappet, applying the air jet through the tappet slot.

Note the number on the ejected adjusting capsule and determine the thickness required for the new capsule, using the clearance measurement taken earlier. Select a new capsule of the correct thickness and fit into the tappet. Remove the holding tool and recheck the clearance. Adjusting capsules are available in different thicknesses, from 3.25 to 4.70 mm, in steps of .05 mm.

1:9 Dismantling the engine

1 Remove the engine and transmission assembly as described in **Section 1:2** and clean as much as possible of the dirt and oil from the engine exterior before proceeding, to prevent contamination of the internal components during dismantling.

2 Separate the gearbox from the engine (see **Chapter 6**). Drain the engine oil from the sump into a suitable container. The drain plug, located in the centre of the sump, is removed by means of a 12 mm Allen key. Remove the dipstick, the alternator and water pump drive belt and all electrical components.

3 Remove the timing belt cover and the timing belt as described in **Section 1:6**, then remove the belt tensioner. Remove the cylinder head assembly, complete with camshaft, as described in **Section 1:3**.

4 Remove the oil filter, fuel pump and the water pump. Remove the distributor, as described in **Chapter 3**.

5 Invert the engine so that it is standing on the cylinder head joint face, then remove the oil sump and gasket. Remove the oil pump and the rear journal oil return pipe, then bend back the locking tab and remove the crankshaft end nut. **FIG 1:19** shows the oil pump and return pipes.

6 Remove the alternator and water pump drive pulley. Remove the toothed pulley from the crankshaft, collecting the key from the shaft.

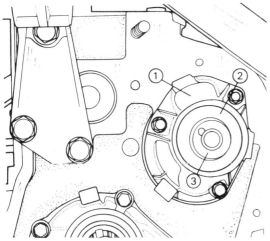

FIG 1:20   The auxiliary shaft flange and seal

7 Bend back the locking tab and remove the fixing screw, then remove the toothed pulley from the auxiliary shaft. Refer to **FIG 1:20** and remove the flange 1 and seal 2 from the auxiliary shaft 3. Remove the distributor and oil pump drive pinion, then remove the auxiliary shaft. If the auxiliary shaft bushes are to be renewed, they must be pressed out with drift A.60372. The new bushes must be pressed in, then reamed with tool A.90365.

8 Remove the flywheel as shown in **FIG 1:21**, marking it to ensure refitting in its original position on the crankshaft flange. Use tool A.60369 or similar to lock the flywheel against rotation.

9 Remove the front and rear crankshaft journal flanges and their seals, the big-end caps and main bearing caps as shown in **FIG 1:22** and collect the thrust washers from the rear main bearing journal as shown in **FIG 1:23**. All of these parts mentioned must be marked to ensure refitting in exactly their original positions. Keep the bearing shells with their appropriate caps for this reason.

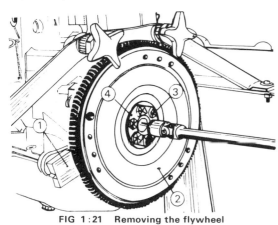

FIG 1:21   Removing the flywheel

Key to Fig 1:21   1 Tool A.60369   2 Flywheel   3 Screws
4 Washer

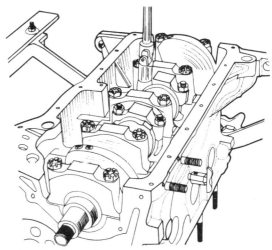

FIG 1:22   Removing the big-end and main bearing caps

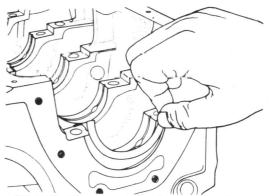

FIG 1:23   The rear main bearing thrust washers

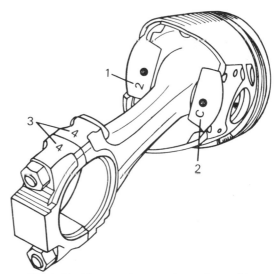

FIG 1:24   Piston and connecting rod assembly

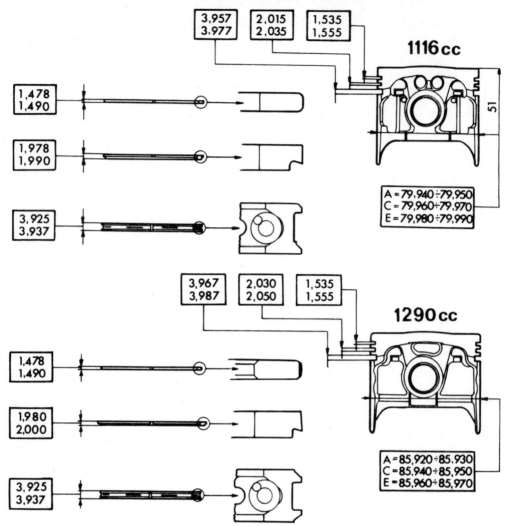

FIG 1:25 Piston ring and groove widths

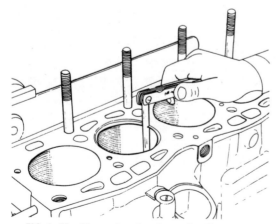

FIG 1:26 Measuring the piston ring fitted gap

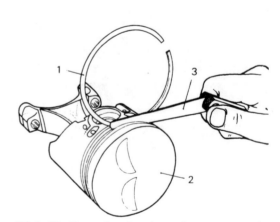

FIG 1:27 Measuring the piston ring to groove clearance

10 Remove the crankshaft and collect the upper main bearing shells, noting their positions. Turn the engine block onto its side, then remove the piston and connecting rod assemblies from the top of their bores, collect the big-end bearing shells from the connecting rods, then store the parts in the correct order for reassembly.

Reassembly:

Reassembly of the engine is a reversal of the dismantling procedure, after servicing the components according to the instructions in the appropriate sections of this chapter. Renew all oil seals and gaskets. During reassembly, all moving parts should be coated with the correct grade of oil, paying particular attention to main and big-end bearings and to the pistons and bores.

1:10 Cylinder block

Thoroughly clean the cylinder block assembly and examine for cracks or other damage. Check the condition of the cylinder walls. If the cylinders are scratched, ovalised or excessively worn, a rebore will be necessary. If the reboring operation would remove too much metal, dry cylinder liners can be fitted. Both the reboring operation and the fitting of dry liners must be carried out by a specialist service station.

1:11 Crankshaft, bearings and flywheel

Crankshaft:

Remove the crankshaft from the engine as described in **Section 1:9** and remove the main and big-end bearings from their respective positions, keeping them in the correct order. If there has been a bearing failure, the crankshaft must be checked for damage and for transfer of metal to its surface. The oilways must be checked to ensure that they are not obstructed. Main and big-end bearing clearance can be checked by the use of Plastigage as described in **Hints on Maintenance and Overhaul** at the end of this manual. If bearing clearance is excessive, the journals should be reground to accept undersize bearing shells, which are available in several different undersizes.

Fit the crankshaft and main bearing assemblies in position, tighten the cap bolts to the specified torque, then use a dial gauge set to the end of the crankshaft to measure the crankshaft end play by levering the shaft backwards and forwards. This play should be between .055 and .265 mm. If end play is greater than this last figure, oversize washers having an extra thickness of .127 mm must be fitted at the rear main bearing position.

Check that the retaining tongue of the bearing is free in its housing and check that the half shells protrude by the same amount on each side of the bearings. When refitting the crankshaft, fit the top half thrust washer in place ensuring that the anti-friction face (with the oil slots) is against the crankshaft shoulder.

Flywheel:

Check the surface of the flywheel which contacts the clutch disc for excessive scoring, which would dictate re-surfacing or renewal. If the starter ring gear must be renewed, this must be carried out with press equipment after heating to 80°C in an oil bath.

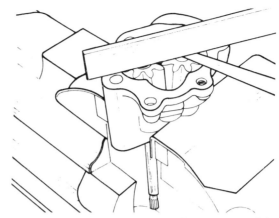

FIG 1:28 Check the pinion to oil pump cover joint face clearance

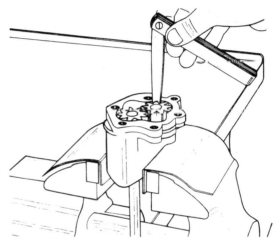

FIG 1:29 Checking oil pump pinion to case clearance

1:12 Pistons and connecting rods:

The removal of the piston from the connecting rod on the 1116 cc engines requires the use of special heating and press equipment, as the gudgeon pin is shrunk-fitted into the small end of the connecting rod, this being a specialist job. However, if piston renewal is not required, all other servicing work can be carried out by the owner in the manner described here.

The small end bushes on 1290 cc engines are a press fit and if they require renewal special tools will be required, the gudgeon pins can be pushed out after removal of the circlips.

Remove the pistons and connecting rods from the engine as described in **Section 1:9. FIG 1:24** shows the piston and connecting rod assembly, with the component identification marks. All components must be refitted in their original positions if they are not to be renewed. **FIG 1:25** shows the thickness measurements for piston rings and ring grooves.

Connecting rods should be inspected for cracks or other damage. Renew any rod found damaged or bent.

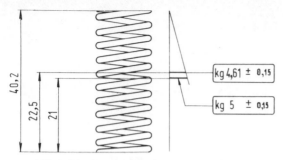

FIG 1:30   Pump spring loads and dimensions

Clean carbon deposits from the piston crowns, remove the rings carefully, then clean carbon from the ring grooves. Inspect the pistons for score marks, signs of seizure and for chipped or worn ring grooves, renewing any piston found to be faulty.

Fit the piston rings one at a time into the bore from which they were removed, pushing them down with the piston crown to ensure squareness. Measure the piston ring fitted gap with feeler gauges as shown in **FIG 1:26** and compare with the figures given in **Technical Data.** If the measurements are at or near the wear limits, new rings must be fitted. Measure the side clearance of the rings in their correct grooves in the piston as shown in **FIG 1:27.** If the wear limit for any ring is reached, the rings and, possibly, the piston must be renewed.

1:13 Lubrication system

Oil pump:

The oil pump may be removed with the engine in the car by supporting the weight of the engine on slings

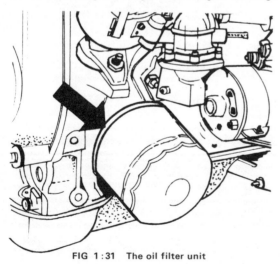

FIG 1:31   The oil filter unit

FIG 1:32   Details of the modified (1972) engine tie-bar

while the crossmember and protection shields are removed. Drain the oil and remove the sump to give access to the pump securing screws.

With the engine removed from the car, proceed with pump removal as described in **Section 1:9.** Use a straightedge and feeler gauges to check the clearance between the top face of the pinions and the pump cover joint face, as shown in **FIG 1:28.** The clearance should be between .020 and .105 mm, with a wear limit of .15 mm. Check the clearance between the periphery of the gears and the side of their housing, as shown in **FIG 1:29.** This should be between .11 and .18 mm with a maximum of .25 mm. Check the length of the spring under the loads shown in **FIG 1:30.** Any part which is worn or damaged must be renewed.

Oil filter:

The external oil filter is of the fullflow type, fitted inside a steel canister, mounted as shown in **FIG 1:31.** The oil filter should be renewed at no more than 10,000 kilometre intervals, or at more frequent intervals if the car is used in dusty or city areas.

To renew the filter, unscrew the old unit from the side of the crankcase, using a strap-type tool if it is stiff to turn. Discard the old unit. Moisten the seal on the new unit with engine oil, then screw it in by hand until the seal just contacts its seat. Now tighten the unit by a further threequarters of a turn. Do not overtighten the unit or leaks may develop.

1:14 Closed crankcase ventilation system

This system operates to draw vapours which form in the crankcase into the air cleaner and carburetter to be harmlessly burned in the engine combustion chambers. Every 20,000 kilometres, the pipes and filters in the system should be removed, flushed with a suitable cleaning solution and refitted.

1:15 New engine tie-bar

From December 1971 the engine tie-bar and mounting bracket on the cylinder head have been modified as shown in **FIG 1:32.**

1:16 Fault diagnosis

(a) Engine will not start

1 Defective coil
2 Faulty distributor capacitor
3 Dirty, pitted or incorrectly set contact points
4 Ignition wires loose or insulation faulty
5 Water on spark plug leads
6 Battery discharged, corrosion of terminals
7 Faulty or jammed starter
8 Sparking plug leads wrongly connected
9 Vapour lock in fuel pipes
10 Defective fuel pump
11 Overchoking or underchoking
12 Blocked fuel filter or carburetter jet
13 Leaking or sticking valves
14 Valve timing incorrect
15 Ignition timing incorrect

(b) Engine stalls

1 Check 1, 2, 3, 4, 5, 10, 11, 12 and 13 in (a)
2 Sparking plugs defective or gaps incorrect
3 Retarded ignition
4 Mixture too weak
5 Water in fuel system
6 Petrol tank vent blocked
7 Incorrect valve clearances

(c) Engine idles badly

1 Check 2 and 7 in (b)
2 Air leak at manifold joints
3 Carburetter adjustment wrong
4 Air leak in carburetter
5 Overrich mixture
6 Worn piston rings
7 Worn valve stems or guides
8 Weak exhaust valve springs

(d) Engine misfires

1 Check 1, 2, 3, 4, 5, 8, 10, 12, 13, 14 and 15 in (a)
2 Weak or broken valve springs

(e) Engine overheats (see Chapter 4)

(f) Compression low

1 Check 13 in (a); 6 and 7 in (c) and 2 in (d)
2 Worn piston ring grooves
3 Scored or worn cylinder bores

(g) Engine lacks power

1 Check 3, 10, 11, 12, 13, 14 and 15 in (a); 2, 3, 4
  and 7 in (b); 6 and 7 in (c) and 2 in (d). Also check
  (e) and (f)
2 Leaking joint washers
3 Fouled spark plugs
4 Automatic advance not working

(h) Burned valves or seats

1 Check 13 and 14 in (a); 7 in (b) and 2 in (d). Also
  check (e)
2 Excessive carbon around valve seats and heads

(j) Sticking valves

1 Check 2 in (d)
2 Bent valve stem
3 Scored valve stem or guide
4 Incorrect valve clearances

(k) Excessive cylinder wear

1 Check 11 in (a)
2 Lack of oil
3 Dirty oil
4 Piston rings gummed up or broken
5 Badly fitting piston rings
6 Bent connecting rod

(l) Excessive oil consumption

1 Check 6 and 7 in (c) and check (k)
2 Ring gaps too wide
3 Oil return holes in piston choked with carbon
4 Scored cylinders
5 Oil level too high
6 External oil leaks

(m) Crankshaft and connecting rod bearing failure

1 Check 2 in (k)
2 Restricted oilways
3 Worn journals or crankpins
4 Loose bearing caps
5 Extremely low oil pressure
6 Bent connecting rod

(n) Internal water leakage (see Chapter 4)

(o) Poor water circulation (see Chapter 4)

(p) Corrosion (see Chapter 4)

(q) High fuel consumption (see Chapter 2)

(r) Engine vibration

1 Loose alternator bolts
2 Engine mountings loose or defective
3 Misfiring due to mixture, ignition or mechanical faults

NOTES

CHAPTER 2

THE FUEL SYSTEM

2:1 Description

A mechanical type fuel pump is used, operated from a cam on the engine auxiliary shaft, as shown in **FIG 2:1**.

The standard carburetter is a single barrel instrument by Weber, Holley or Solex, with a diaphragm type economizer device. Later high performance cars are equipped with a double barrelled Weber carburetter.

Paper cartridge type air cleaner units are used, fitted to the carburetter intake. The air cleaner housing is provided with two alternative intakes, controlled by a lever on the side of the housing, to allow heated or cold air to be drawn into the carburetter according to the season of the year.

2:2 Air cleaner

Every 10,000 kilometres the air cleaner element should be renewed in the following manner. If the car is operated under very dusty conditions, the servicing periods should be halved. Refer to **FIG 2:2** and remove the wingnuts **A** to release the cover **B**. Lift off the cover and remove the element **C**. Wipe the inside of the air cleaner housing and cover to remove any grease or dirt, then fit a new element and replace the cover.

During warm summer weather, the air cleaner intake air should be drawn from the cool intake, during cold winter weather from the warm intake. Press the knob **D** shown in **FIG 2:3** inwards, then move it to the appropriate position. **F** shows the position for the admission of cool air in summer, **G** the position for warm air admission during winter.

2:3 Fuel pump

Testing:

Before testing the pump, ensure that the fuel tank vent system is not blocked. If it is suspected that fuel is not reaching the carburetter, disconnect the carburetter feed pipe and hold a suitable container under the end of the pipe. Turn the engine over a few times with the starter and watch for fuel squirting from the end of the pipe, which indicates that the pump is working. If so, check the float needle in the carburetter for possible sticking.

Reduced fuel flow can be caused by blocked fuel pipes or a clogged filter. Check the filter elements in the fuel pump and carburetter. If an obstructed pipeline appears to be the cause of the trouble, it may be cleared with compressed air. Disconnect the pipeline at the pump and

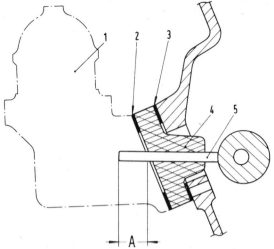

FIG 2:1   Fuel pump operation

Key to Fig 2:1   1 Fuel pump   **2, 3** Gaskets   **4** Pump support   **5** Pump pushrod   **A**=Pump stroke of 15 mm

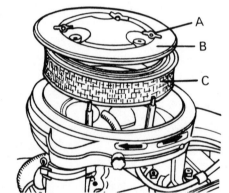

FIG 2:2   Removing the air cleaner filter element

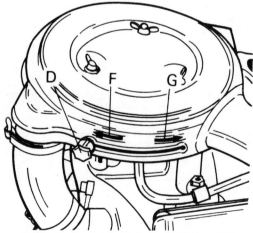

FIG 2:3   The intake air temperature control

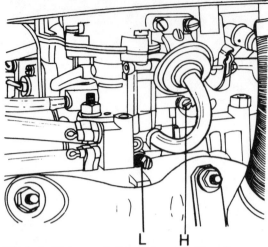

FIG 2:4   Weber or Holley carburetter idle adjustment screws

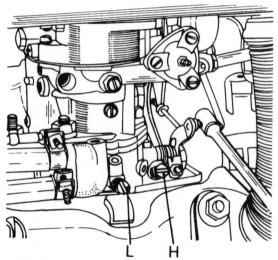

FIG 2:5   Solex carburetter idle adjustment screws

carburetter. **Do not pass compressed air through the pump or the valves will be damaged.** If there is an obstruction between the pump and the tank, remove the tank filler cap before blowing the pipe through from the pump end.

If the pump delivers insufficient fuel, suspect an air leak between the pump and the tank, dirt under the pump valves or faulty valve seatings. If no fuel is delivered, suspect a sticking valve or a faulty pump diaphragm.

Servicing:

Disconnect the fuel pipes from the fuel pump and fit plugs to the pipes to prevent fuel loss before removing the pump from the vehicle. As the pump valves are crimped into the pump body they cannot be renewed separately, so faulty valves which cannot be corrected by washing in petrol to remove dirt will dictate renewal of the unit.

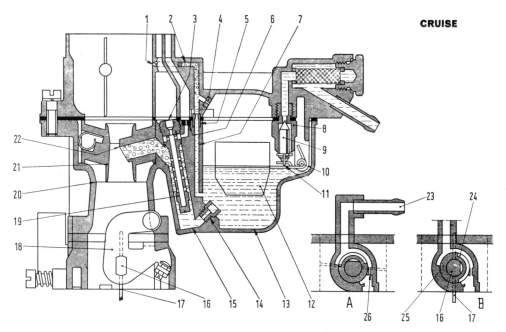

ACCELERATING PUMP

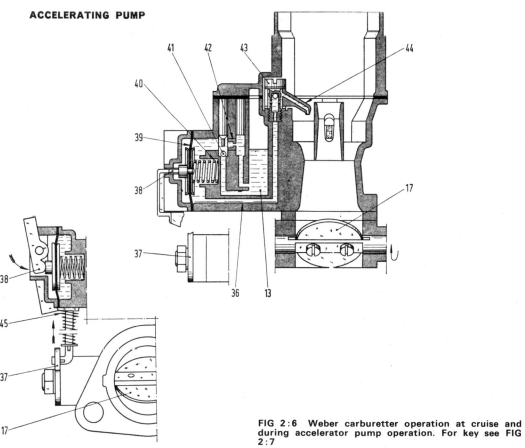

FIG 2:6 Weber carburetter operation at cruise and during accelerator pump operation. For key see FIG 2:7

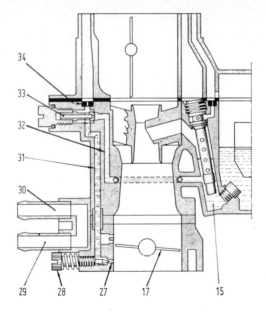

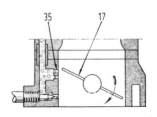

IDLE AND TRANSFER

CHOKE

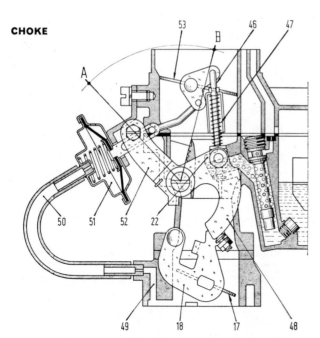

FIG 2:7 Weber carburetter operation on idle and transfer and choke operation

Key to Figs 2:6 and 2:7   1 Power fuel calibrated orifice   2 Power mixture passage   3 Bleeding air jet
4 Air intake calibrated orifice   5 Power fuel calibrated bushing   6 Air intake calibrated bushing   7 Lower fuel passage
8 Needle valve   9 Valve needle   10 Float hinge pin   11 Needle return hook to float tang   12 Float   13 Bowl   14 Main jet
15 Emulsion tube well   16 Throttle shaft   17 Throttle valve   18 Crankcase gas suction device control lever   19 Emulsion tube
20 Primary venturi   21 Auxiliary venturi   22 Spray tube   23 Blow-by gas duct   24 Slot for blow-by gas flow when cruising
25 Rotary valve   26 Calibrated orifice for blow-by gas suction at idle   27 Idle feed orifice   28 Idle adjusting screw
29, 30 Water ducts for heating idle passage area   31 Idle passage   32 Fuel passage   33 Idle jet   34 Idle air calibrated bushing
35 Idle transfer orifices   36 Delivery passage   37 Throttle control lever   38 Accelerating pump control lever   39 Diaphragm
40 Suction spring   41 Ball valve   42 Excess fuel recirculation bushing from accelerating pump   43 Delivery valve
44 Accelerating pump nozzle   45 Throttle cushion spring   46 Rod   47 Calibrated spring   48 Lobe   49 Vacuum passage
50 Vacuum tube   51 Diaphragm device   52 Choke control lever   53 Choke

28

Test the action of the valves by blowing and sucking at the inlet and outlet points. It should be possible to blow air in through the pump inlet but not to suck air out, and it should be possible to suck air out of the pump outlet but not to blow air in. If the valves do not work properly according to this test, then a new unit must be fitted.

Check the pump diaphragm for splits, distortion or hardening of the material. If it is not in perfect condition, a new diaphragm should be fitted.

The gasket at 2 (see **FIG 2:1**) must always be .3 mm thick, the gasket at 3 is supplied in thicknesses of .3 mm, .7 mm and 1.2 mm to enable the pump stroke of 15 to 15.5 mm **A** in **FIG 2:1** to be obtained.

2:4 Carburetter adjustments

Slow-running adjustments described in this section should be carried out after any carburetter, ignition system or valve clearance adjustments or servicing have been made, or at any time if engine idling is rough or at too high a speed. It must be pointed out, however, that these adjustments will only be effective if the sparking plugs and ignition system are in good order, and that the engine must be at normal operating temperature when they are carried out.

Refer to **FIG 2:4** for Weber or Holley carburetters, **FIG 2:5** for Solex carburetters. With the engine at normal operating temperature, screw in the throttle stop screw **H** until a fast idle of about 1000 rev/min is achieved. If the engine cuts when the throttle is released, tighten the screw **H** half a turn at a time between re-starts until the engine will remain running at the fast idle stated.

With the engine running at fast idle, turn the idle mixture screw **L** slowly in or out as required, to obtain the fastest possible idle under these conditions. Now screw out the throttle stop screw **H** to slow the idle to about 850 rev/min, making further very fine adjustments to the idle mixture screw if necessary, to obtain a smooth, slow idle.

This done, open the throttle sharply a few times to raise the engine speed, allowing the throttle to return to the rest position under its own spring action. Check that the engine returns to the original smooth idle after throttle release. If the engine tends to cut when the throttle is opened sharply, unscrew the idle mixture screw **L** a quarter turn at a time and recheck. If the engine cuts when the throttle is released, screw in the throttle stop screw a quarter turn at a time until cutting is eliminated, then readjust the idle as previously described. If the engine returns to a higher idling speed than was set, check that the throttle linkage is returning completely to its stop. If so, screw out the throttle stop screw **H** to slow the idle sufficiently, then recheck. If the linkage does not return fully, check for binding or obstructions and lubricate all pivots and joints between the accelerator pedal and carburetter. Check also that the throttle linkage return spring is properly located and that it has not weakened.

2:5 Weber and Holley carburetters

In this section, the descriptions and servicing instructions are given for Weber units in the 32.ICEV series, the design and operation of Holley units being similar in all respects.

Operation:

Normal running at cruise:

Refer to **FIGS 2:6** and **2:7**. Fuel flows through the needle valve into the float chamber 13 where the float 12, mounted on the pivot 10 regulates the needle valve 9 opening to keep the fuel at a constant correct level. From the float chamber 13 the fuel passes through the main jet 14 to the well 15. After mixing with the air coming from air jets 3 and air bleed 6 through the ejector tube 22 and emulsion tube 19, the fuel reaches the carburetion zone formed by the choke tube 20 and emulsion block 21.

The carburetter enrichment system operates in the following manner: From float chamber 13 through channel 7 and calibrated ring 5 the fuel mixes with the air coming from the calibrated hole 4. This mixture passes through channel 2 and is injected through calibrated hole 1 into the carburetter during high speed operation of the engine.

The illustration also shows the crankcase fumes re-circulation system, diagrams **A** and **B**. The recirculation system consists of a revolving shutter 25 driven by shaft 16, which is controlled by lever 18 which, through groove 24, connects tube 23 with the zone below the butterfly valve 17. Even when the butterfly valve is in the idling position a certain amount of recirculation occurs through calibrated hole 26.

Idling and progression:

From the well 15 fuel flows to the idle jet 33 through channel 32. Mixing with the air supplied by air bleed 34 through channel 31 and idle hole 27 (adjustable by screw 28) fuel reaches the carburetter conduit below the butterfly 17.

With the progressive opening of the butterfly as the throttle is opened, the mixture flows through the progression hole 35, thus allowing a progressive regular increase of the engine speed. To avoid freezing of the idling zone and progression holes, hot water drawn from the engine cooling circuit flows through tubes 29 and 30, which are connected in parallel and maintains the idling zone at a warm temperature.

Acceleration:

Opening the butterfly valve 17 which is operated by lever 37, ring 45 and lever 38, causes the diaphragm 39 to inject fuel into the carburetter conduit through channel 36, valve 43 and emulsion block 44 of the pump jet. Spring 45 damps the sudden opening of the butterfly 17 and prolongs the fuel output. The excess fuel supplied by the accelerator pump returns to float chamber 13 through the calibrated ring 42. When the butterfly 17 returns to the closed position, lever 38 frees the diaphragm which, under the action of spring 40, draws fuel through the ball valves 41 and refills the chamber.

Cold starting:

When lever 52 is in position A, valve 53 closes the air inlet whilst butterfly valve 17, operated by cam 48, lever 52 and lever 18, opens partially. This is the fast idling position. Emulsion block 22 then supplies a fuel mixture which permits prompt starting of the engine. When the engine starts, the vacuum caused partially opens valve 53 against the calibrated spring 47. The vacuum below butterfly valve 17 through channel 49

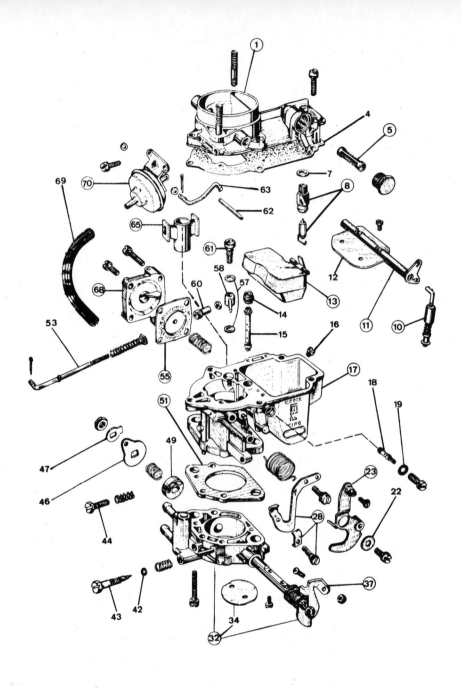

FIG 2:8   Weber carburetter components, manual choke type

Key to Fig 2:8   1 Float chamber cover   4 Gasket   5 Filter   7 Washer   8 Needle valve   10 Choke control link
11 Choke valve spindle   12 Choke valve   13 Float   14 Air correction jet   15 Emulsion tube   16 Main jet   17 Body
18 Idling jet   19 Washer   22 Washer   23 Choke control lever   28 Control cable bracket   32 Throttle body
34 Throttle valve   37 Throttle control and spindle   42 Seal   43 Volume control screw   44 Slow-running screw
46 Accelerator pump lever   47 Tab washer   49 Oil vapour recirculating valve   51 Flange   53 Accelerator pump rod
55 Diaphragm   57 Washers   58 Discharge tube   60 Accelerator pump stroke adjusting nut   61 Check valve
62 Float spindle   63 Depression system choke control rod   65 Small venturi   68 Accelerator pump cover   69 Depression
system tube   70 Depression diaphragm chamber

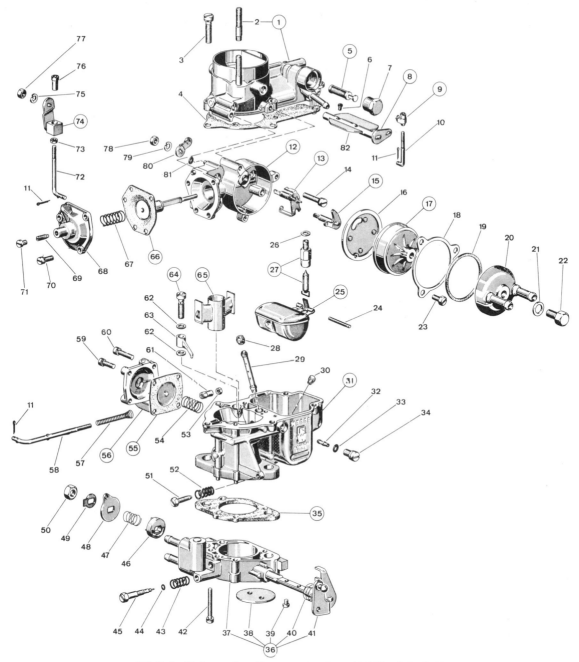

FIG 2:9   Weber carburetter components, automatic choke type

Key to Fig 2:9   1 Float chamber cover assembly   2 Stud   3 Bolt   4 Gasket   5 Filter   6 Screw   7 Filter inspection plug
8 Choke spindle   9 Adjuster   10 Choke control link   11 Splitpin   12 Automatic choke assembly   13 Automatic choke lever
assembly   14 Bolt   15 Link   16 Thermostat unit seal   17 Automatic choke thermostatic spring assembly   18 Thermostat
retainer   19 Seal   20 Coolant chamber   21 Seal   22 Bolt   23 Screw   24 Float pin   25 Float   26 Washer   27 Needle
valve   28 Air correction jet   29 Emulsion tube   30 Main jet   31 Carburetter body   32 Idling jet   33 Washer   34 Jet carrier
35 Insulating flange   36 Carburetter throttle assembly   37 Base unit   38 Throttle valve   39 Screw   40 Throttle spindle
41 Throttle lever   42 Screw   43 Spring   44 Seal   45 Volume control (mixture) screw   46 Oil vapour recirculating valve
47 Spring   48 Accelerator pump lever   49 Tabwasher   50 Nut   51 Idle speed screw   52 Spring   53 Nut   54 Spring
55 Accelerator pump diaphragm   56 Pump cover   57 Spring   58 Accelerator pump rod   59 Screw   60 Screw   61 Accelerator
pump stroke adjuster   62 Washer   63 Discharge tube   64 Check valve   65 Venturi   66 Vacuum dechoke diaphragm   67 Spring
68 Vacuum unit cover   69 Dechoke adjuster   70 Screw   71 Screw   72 Fast-idle control rod   73 Nut   74 Choke control lever
75 Spring washer   76 Adjuster   77 Nut   78 Nut   79 Spring washer   80 Automatic choke lever   81 Seal   82 Choke valve

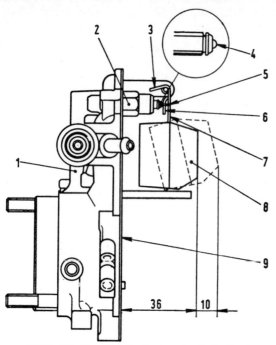

FIG 2:10 Float level adjustment, plastic float

Key to Fig 2:10   1 Carburetter cover   2 Needle valve
3 Lug   4 Movable ball   5 Return hook   6 Tang
7 Float arm   8 Float   9 Gasket

damage or enlarge the jets. If a jet has a blockage which cannot be cleared with compressed air, use a single bristle from a stiff brush for the purpose. If this method is unsuccessful, renew the jet. Details of jet sizes are given in **Technical Data** in the **Appendix**.

Make sure that all sediment is cleared from the float chamber and inspect the float for damage or leakage, either of which will dictate renewal of the float assembly. Float leakage can usually be detected by shaking the float and listening for the sound of fuel splash inside.

Check the float needle valve assembly carefully, renewing the assembly if there is any sign of a ridge on the tapered valve seat. A damaged needle valve can lead to flooding by failing to cut off the fuel supply properly when the float chamber is full, or may stick in the closed position and prevent sufficient fuel from reaching the float chamber.

Examine the carburetter filter and renew it if it is deformed or damaged, or if it will not clean up successfully.

On completion, reassemble the carburetter in the reverse order of dismantling, using new gaskets throughout. Take care not to overtighten the jets or component fixing screws to avoid stripping the threads in the light alloy castings. During the reassembly procedure, carry out the float levelling operations described next. These done and the carburetter fully assembled, refit to the car and reconnect the hoses and the linkages, making sure that the linkages operate smoothly and open and close the throttle and choke completely. Finally, carry out the slow-running adjustments described in **Section 2:4**.

Float level adjustments:

Refer to **FIG 2:10**. With the needle valve assembly 2 firmly tightened onto its seat and the ball 4 free in its housing, hold the carburetter cover vertically as shown so that the weight of the float 8 holds the needle valve closed but does not press the ball 4 into the needle valve.

Under these conditions the float level must be 36 mm, measured between the bottom of the float and the joint face of the carburetter cover with the gasket fitted to the cover. Adjust the float level if necessary by carefully bending the small tag which contacts the ball 4.

After correcting the float level, check that the float stroke is 10 mm (8.5 mm on type 32.ICEV.10), adjusting to obtain this figure by carefully bending lug 3. Check that the return hook 5 permits free movement of the needle valve in its seat. On completion, refit the carburetter cover to the carburetter and check that the float moves freely without touching the sides of the float chamber.

The above details refer to plastic floats. When a metal float is fitted, the float level is 11 mm and the float travel is 7 mm. These measurements must be taken from the top of the float to the cover gasket and not to the bottom of the float as with plastic floats.

Gauge A95136 should be used for later carburetters.

2:6 Solex carburetters

The design and operation of the Solex carburetter is similar to the Weber carburetter described in **Section 2:5**. Carburetter servicing should be carried out as described in **Section 2:5**, dismantling the assembly into the order shown in **FIG 2:11**.

Gauge A95135 is required for float level adjustment.

and tube 50 acts on the diaphragm 51 and causes the mixture to become leaner for irregular speed operation of the engine. When the engine has warmed up sufficiently, the driver can return the choke control to the off position setting the linkage to position B, valve 53 being kept fully open by rod 46 while the butterfly rod 70 returns to the normal idling position.

On some estate models an automatic choke is fitted, in which case a temperature sensitive spring (contained in the drum 17 in **FIG 2:9**) regulates the operation according to coolant temperature without the need for manual control.

Carburetter servicing:

To remove the carburetter, remove the air cleaner cover and filter element, then remove the cleaner body from the carburetter. Disconnect the hoses and the throttle and choke linkages. Remove the mounting nuts and lift the carburetter from the manifold.

Dismantle the carburetter into the order shown in **FIG 2:8** or **2:9**, carefully noting the positions of the components, laying them out on a clean sheet of paper. Mark shafts, levers and butterfly valves so that they will be reassembled in the correct relative positions. Use the correct size of screwdriver when removing jets, to avoid damage.

Clean all parts in petrol or an approved carburetter cleaner, then examine them for wear or damage. Renew any faulty parts. Clean jets and passages thoroughly, using compressed air, clean petrol and a small, stiff brush. **Do not use cloth for cleaning purposes, as small fibres may remain after cleaning and clog the jets or passages. Never use a wire probe as this will**

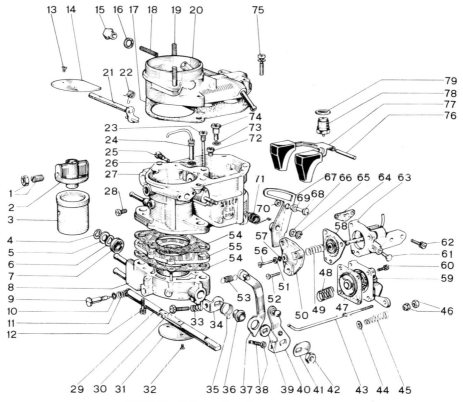

FIG 2:11 Solex carburetter components

Key to Fig 2:11   1 Grubscrew and locknut   2 Delivery venturi   3 Main venturi   4 Spring clip   5 Distance piece
6 Wave washer   7 Oil recirculation valve   8 Heated throttle housing   9 Volume control screw   10 Seal   11 Spring
12 Screw and spring washer   13 Screw   14 Choke plate   15 Filter plug   16 Plug seal   17 Gasket   18 Filter
19 Stud   20 Float chamber cover   21 Choke valve spindle   22 Spindle spring   23 Diffuser   24 Accelerator pump
delivery plate and injector   25 Idle jet   26 Seal   27 Carburetter body   28 Venturi lockscrew   29 Throttle spindle
30 Slow-running adjustment screw   31 Throttle plate   32 Screw   33 Spring   34 Throttle stop lever   35 Spring
36 Fast-idle lever bush and distance piece   37 Fast-idle lever   38 Fast-idle adjusting screw and locknut   39 Washer
40 Throttle lever   41 Washer   42 Nut   43 Accelerator pump operating rod   44 Washer   45 Spring   46 Adjusting nut
and locknut   47 Accelerator pump diaphragm   48 Spring   49 Spring   50 Econostat cover   51 Locknut   52 Screw
53 Spring   54 Gaskets   55 Insulating flange   56 Econostat adjustment screw   57 Seal   58 Diaphragm
59 Accelerator pump cover   60 Screw and spring washer   61 Screw   62 Screw and spring washer   63 Econostat body
64 Gasket   65 Spring clip   66 Washer   67 Choke lever   68 Clamp screw   69 Bush   70 Nut   71 Spring
72 Main jet   73 Seal   74 Accelerator pump valve   75 Float chamber cover securing screw and washer   76 Float spindle
77 Float   78 Needle valve   79 Washer

2:7 Weber carburetter type 32 DMTR

Towards the end of 1972 some high performance cars were added to the 128 range, designated 128 Rally, 128S and 128SL and more recently the 3P. These cars are equipped with a double barrelled carburetter of the above mentioned type. The S and SL models have carburetter type No. 32.DMTR.20, the 3P models have type 32.DMTR. 32, while the Rally version has a 32.DMTR or 32.DMTR.20 which also includes provision for blow-by gas re-intake and, in order to comply with certain overseas regulations, arrangements to reduce carbon monoxide emissions at idling speeds, these include a factory sealed throttle stop screw.

The fuel supply system to the carburetter is also modified to include a pipe to return excess fuel at the carburetter to the tank.

A manually operated choke is used to obtain the rich mixture required for cold start, but a vacuum controlled device is included the purpose of which is to open the eccentrically pivoted choke plate according to the depression obtaining in the manifold and so prevent over-choking.

A differential mechanism is used to link the two throttles so that the greater part of normal part-throttle running is done with only the primary throttle in operation. This ensures economical running, as the secondary barrel is in use only for open throttle work when maximum performance is required.

Operation:

Starting. Reference to **FIG 2:12** shows the linkage by which the manual control is coupled to the spring

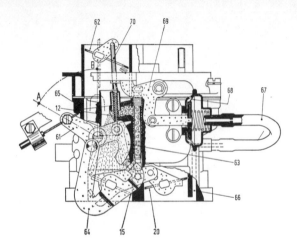

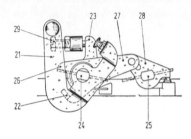

FIG 2:13 Throttle plate differential opening system

Key to Figs 2:11, 2:12 and 2:13   12 Jet tube
15 Main throttle butterfly   16 Emulsion tube   18 Main jet
well   20 Secondary throttle butterfly   21 Throttle butterfly
control lever   22 Lug   23 Quadrant on main shaft   24 Main
shaft   25 Secondary shaft   26 Lug on idle lever   27 Idle
lever   28 Secondary throttle butterfly shaft control lever
29 Main throttle butterfly positioning bolt and locknut   34 Main
idling jet   35 Idling fuel duct   36 Idling air calibrated orifice
37 Main idling fuel duct   38 Idling air calibrated orifice
39 Idling mixture calibrated plug   40 Idling mixture screw
41 Bypass idling duct   42 Bypass idling duct calibrated
orifice   43 Bypass idling air orifice   44 Bypass idling
adjusting screw   45 Bypass idling mixture inlet duct
46 Main duct progressive orifices   47 Secondary well
48 Secondary idling jet   49 Secondary duct air calibrated
orifice   50 Fuel duct   51 Secondary duct progressive orifices
61 Choke operating lever   62 Choke flap   63 Main throttle
butterfly opening cam (fast idling)   64 Throttle butterfly
lever   65 Rated spring   66 Vacuum spring   67 Vacuum pipe
68 Vacuum diaphragm system to partially open flap 62 69 Choke
flap control lever   70 Choke flap link

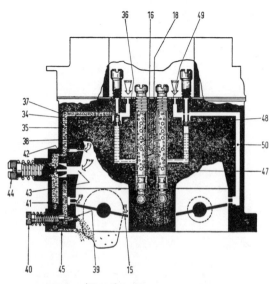

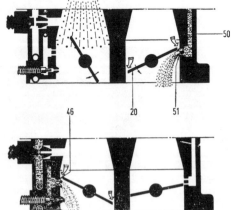

FIG 2:12 Operation of Weber type 32.DMTR carburetter. Top to bottom: choke system, idle, secondary
barrel progression, primary barrel progression

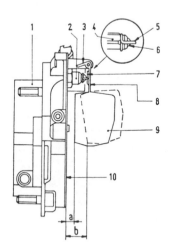

FIG 2:14 Setting the float level

Key to Fig 2:14   a=6 mm   b=15 mm
1 Carburetter float chamber   2 Needle valve seat   3 Lug
4 Needle valve   5 Return hook   6 Movable ball   7 Tab
8 Float arm   9 Float   10 Gasket

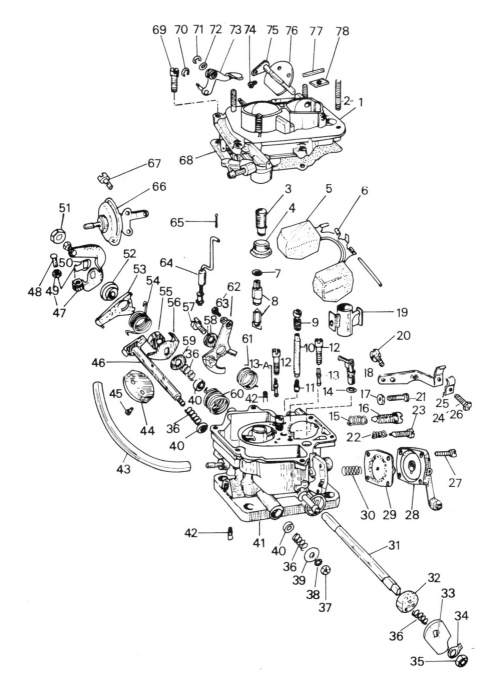

FIG 2:15   Components of Weber carburetter type 32.DMTR

Key to Fig 2:15   1 Float chamber   3 Filter   5 Float   6 Float pivot   7 Seal   8 Needle valve   9 Air compensator jet
10 Emulsion tube   11 Main jet (1 primary, 1 secondary)   13 and 13a Primary and secondary idling jets   14 Seal   16 Bypass
idling adjustment screw   18 Accelerator pump injector   19 Auxiliary diffuser   23 Minimum idling speed adjusting screw
24 Choke flap cable cover clamp   28 Accelerating pump cover   29 Accelerating pump diaphragm   31 Primary throttle
butterfly shaft   32 Oil vapour re-intake distributor   33 Accelerating pump control cam   34 and 50 Tab washers   40 Bush
41 Float chamber body   43 Vacuum pipe   44 Throttle butterfly   46 Secondary throttle butterfly shaft   47 Throttle butterfly
shaft control   52 Shouldered washer   53 Hang up lever   55 Spring guide bush   56 Secondary shaft control lever
62 Initial opening lever   64 Choke flap control link   66 Choke weakening system   68 Carburetter float chamber gasket
73 Weakening system control lever   75 Choke flap shaft   76 Choke flap   77 Plate retaining bar   78 Dust cover plate

loaded choke plate and also the mechanism by which the primary throttle is given a small opening when the choke is fully closed. By this means a suitably rich mixture is obtained for a fast-idle when warming up.

The diagram also shows the vacuum capsule and linkage by which the amount of choking is reduced when over-high depression is forming in the inlet manifold.

Idling and progression:

It will be seen from **FIG 2:12** that the idling circuit is very similar to that in the Weber carburetter described earlier, in that the idle mixture is metered through passages in the carburetter body with a fully closed throttle plate (see **FIG 2:7**).

Similarly it is shown in the bottom diagram that progression from idle to part throttle operation is the same as on the earlier type of carburetter.

The centre diagram shows how the secondary barrel commences to come into operation at about two thirds throttle. A smooth progression to two barrelled operation is ensured by first uncovering the secondary progression holes which perform the same service as the equivalent holes in the primary barrel.

Acceleration:

A similar type of accelerator pump is used on the 32.DMTR carburetter as on the 32.ICEV, also a similar method of consuming the crankcase fumes.

Cruising:

The operation of the carburetter when cruising normally is the same as with the earlier type, but with the addition of the extra fuel supplied by the secondary barrel when the primary throttle is more than two thirds open.

The mechanism by which this differential throttle opening is obtained may be seen in **FIG 2:13**. The linkage is also so arranged that the two throttle plates reach the fully open position simultaneously.

Float level adjustment:

The action of the float/needle-valve assembly is similar, but different dimensions are involved as may be seen from **FIG 2:14**.

With the float chamber cover held in the vertical position as shown, the two dimensions a and b are as follows:

a = the distance between the float and the float chamber cover gasket face with the gasket in position and the needle valve held lightly closed.

b = the maximum distance between the float and the gasket face.

b−a = the total float travel.

a = 6 mm   b = 15 mm   b−a = 9 mm

The components of the carburetter are shown in the exploded diagram **FIG 2:15**.

2:8 Fault diagnosis

(a) Leakage or insufficient fuel delivered

1 Air vent to tank restricted
2 Fuel pipes blocked
3 Air leaks at pipe connections
4 Fuel filter blocked
5 Pump gaskets faulty
6 Pump diaphragm defective
7 Pump valves sticking or seating badly

(b) Excessive fuel consumption

1 Carburetter requires adjustment
2 Fuel leakage
3 Sticking mixture control
4 Float level too high
5 Dirty air cleaner
6 Worn jets in carburetter
7 Excessive engine temperature
8 Idling speed too high

(c) Idling speed too high

1 Rich fuel mixture
2 Throttle control sticking
3 Choke control sticking
4 Worn throttle valves

(d) Noisy fuel pump

1 Loose pump mountings
2 Air leaks on suction side of diaphragm
3 Obstruction in fuel pipeline
4 Clogged fuel filter

(e) No fuel delivery

1 Float needle valve stuck
2 Tank vent system blocked
3 Defective pump diaphragm
4 Pump valve stuck
5 Pipeline obstructed
6 Bad air leak on suction side of pump

CHAPTER 3

THE IGNITION SYSTEM

3:1 Description

A conventional coil ignition system is employed consisting of a 12-volt negative earth battery, coil and distributor/contact breaker assembly. In order to ensure that the spark occurs at the optimum piston position the distributor includes a centrifugal mechanism to advance the firing point relative to the engine speed. As the engine speed increases two spring loaded weights, attached to the contact breaker cam, are thrown outwards by centrifugal action and progressively move the cam in the appropriate direction to advance the ignition timing. The standard distributor is a Marelli, although some early cars may have a Ducellier. Both types are shown in exploded form in FIG 3:3, from which it will be seen that they are similar in construction and operation.

The ignition coil is wound as an auto-transformer, with the primary and secondary windings connected in series, the common junction being connected to the contact breaker with the positive feed from the battery going to the opposite terminal of the LT winding, via the ignition switch.

When the contacts are closed, current flows in the coil primary winding, magnetizing the core and setting up a fairly strong magnetic field. Each time the contacts open, the battery current is cut off and the magnetic field collapses, inducing a high current in the primary winding and a high voltage in the secondary. The primary current is used to charge the capacitor connected across the contacts and the flow is high and virtually instantaneous. It is this high current peak which induces the surge in the secondary winding to produce the sparking voltage across the plug points. Without the capacitor, the current peak would be much smaller and the sparking voltage considerably reduced, in fact to a point where it would be insufficient to fire the mixture in the engine cylinders. The capacitor, therefore, serves the dual purpose of minimizing contact breaker wear and providing the necessary high charging surge to ensure a powerful spark.

3:2 Routine maintenance

Pull off the two spring clips and remove the distributor cap. Apply a small drop of oil to the moving parts of the contact breaker assembly and, if a felt lubricating pad is fitted, apply just enough oil to soak it, as shown in FIG 3:1. Apply a thin smear of grease to the cam which opens the points. When lubricating the internal parts of

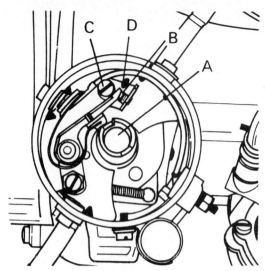

FIG 3:1   Adjusting the contact breaker points

Key to Fig 3:1   A Felt wick   B Contact points gap
C Clamp screw   D Adjustment slot

the distributor, take great care to avoid oil or grease contaminating the contact breaker points, lubricating sparingly for this reason.

Adjusting the contact breaker points:

Turn the engine until one of the cams has opened the contact breaker points to their fullest extent, then check the gap between the points with clean feeler gauges. The correct gap is between .37 and .43 mm for Marelli distributors and .45 mm for Ducellier units. To adjust the gap, loosen the contact point clamp screws and move the fixed contact point until the gap is correct, as shown in **FIG 3:1**. Tighten the screws and recheck the gap.

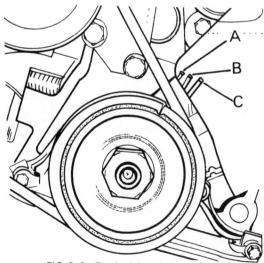

FIG 3:2   The ignition timing marks

Key to Fig 3:2   A 10 degrees   B 5 degrees   C 0 degrees

Cleaning the contact points:

Use a fine carborundum stone or special contact file to polish the points if they are dirty or pitted, taking care to keep the faces flat and square. If the points are too worn to clean up in this manner, they should be renewed. On completion of cleaning, wipe away all dust with a cloth moistened in petrol.

3:3 Ignition faults

If the engine runs unevenly, set it to idle at about 1000 rev/min and, taking care not to touch any conducting part of the sparking plug leads, remove and replace each lead from its plug in turn. To avoid shocks during this operation, it is best to wear a pair of thick gloves or to use insulated pliers. Doing this to a plug which is firing correctly will accentuate the uneven running but will make no difference if the plug is not firing.

Having by this means located the faulty cylinder, stop the engine and remove the plug lead. Pull back the insulation or remove the connector so that the end of the lead is exposed. Start the engine and hold the lead carefully to avoid shocks so that the end is about $\frac{1}{8}$ inch away from the cylinder head. A strong, regular spark confirms that the fault lies with the sparking plug which should be removed and cleaned as described in **Section 3:6**, or renewed if defective.

If the spark is weak and irregular, check the condition of the lead and, if it is perished or cracked, renew it and repeat the test. If no improvement results, check that the inside of the distributor cap is clean and dry and that there is no sign of 'tracking', which can be seen as a thin black line between the electrodes, or to some metal part in contact with the cap. 'Tracking' can only be cured by fitting a new cap. Check also that the contact in the centre of the cap touches the contact at the centre of the rotor. The contact in the cap should be in good condition and move freely against its internal spring.

Testing the low-tension circuit:

Check that the contact breaker points are clean and correctly set, then proceed as follows:

Remove the sparking plugs. Disconnect the thin wire from the coil that leads to the distributor. Connect a 12-volt test lamp between these terminals, switch on the ignition and turn the engine slowly by hand pressure on the drive belt. If, when the contact points close the lamp lights and when they open the lamp goes out, the circuit is in order. If the lamp fails to light, there is a fault in the low-tension circuit.

If the fault lies in the low-tension circuit, use the test lamp to carry out the following tests, with the ignition switched on.

Remove the wire from the ignition switch side of the coil and connect the lamp between the end of this wire and earth. If the lamp fails to light it indicates a fault in the wiring or connections between the battery and the coil, or in the ignition switch. Reconnect the wire if the lamp lights.

Disconnect the wire from the coil that leads to the distributor. Connect the lamp between the coil terminal and earth. If the lamp fails to light it indicates a fault in the primary winding and a new coil must be fitted.

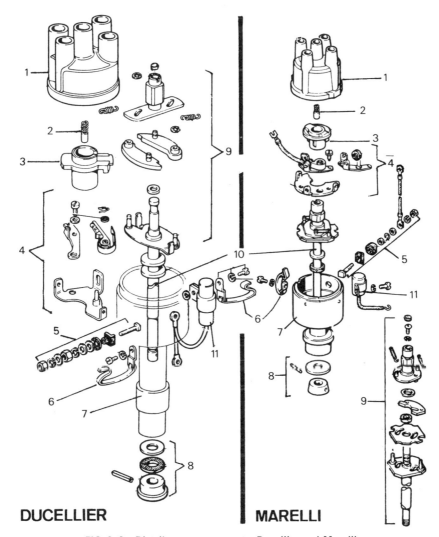

FIG 3:3   Distributor components, Ducellier and Marelli

Key to Fig 3:3   1 Distributor cap   2 Rotor contact brush   3 Rotor   4 Contact breaker assembly   5 Low-tension wire
connection   6 Cap retaining clip   7 Distributor body   8 Distributor drive components   9 Cam and centrifugal advance
mechanism   10 Distributor shaft   11 Capacitor

Reconnect the wire if the lamp lights and disconnect its other end from the distributor. If the lamp does not light when connected between the end of the wire and earth, it indicates a fault in that section of wire.

Capacitor:

The best method of testing a capacitor is by substitution. Disconnect the original capacitor and connect a new one between the low-tension terminal on the distributor and earth, for test purposes. If a new capacitor is proved to be required, it can then be properly fitted. The capacitor is of .22 to .23 microfarad capacity.

3:4 Removing and dismantling distributor

Removal:

Turn the engine until No. 1 cylinder is at TDC on the firing stroke, No. 1 being the cylinder nearest the timing gear end of the engine. To do this, remove the distributor cap and turn the engine until the rotor points towards the cap segment for No. 1 cylinder, or turn the engine until both valves in No. 1 cylinder are closed. This done, turn the engine a little more as necessary until the timing notch in the crankshaft pulley aligns with the 10 deg. advance mark on the front of the timing gear cover on the engine, as shown in **FIG 3:2**.

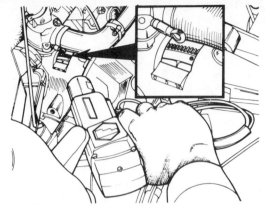

FIG 3:4 Checking the ignition timing with a strobo-scopic lamp on the flywheel

Remove the distributor cap. Disconnect the low-tension wire from the distributor. Note the position of the rotor relative to the distributor body and mark the position of the distributor body relative to the engine block. Undo the body clamp and pull the distributor out of the engine block. Do not turn the engine at all while the distributor is removed, otherwise the timing marks will have to be realigned for refitting.

Refitting:

With the timing marks aligned correctly as previously described, offer the distributor into position with the mark on the body aligned with the mark on the engine block. Turn the rotor to the position noted during removal and push the distributor down into position, noting that the rotor may have to be turned a fraction to allow the drive mechanism to mesh with the gear on the engine auxiliary shaft. When the distributor seats the rotor must be correctly pointing towards the cap segment for firing No. 1 cylinder. Tighten the distributor clamp. If necessary, check the ignition timing as described in **Section 3:5.**

Dismantling:

Pull off the rotor from the top of the cam, Using a suitable punch, drive out the retaining pin from the drive dog and remove the drive dog and washers. Withdraw the shaft assembly from the body, collecting the washers. Loosen the terminal screw on the contact breaker and disconnect the leads, then remove the contact breaker assembly. **FIG 3:3** shows the distributor components.

Thoroughly clean all parts in petrol or carbon tetra-chloride and dry them. Examine for wear or damage and renew parts as necessary. Clean and examine the contact breaker points. If they are slightly burned or pitted, polish them as described in **Section 3:2** or, if the wear is excessive, fit a new contact point set.

When inspection and servicing has been completed, reassemble the distributor in the reverse order of dis-mantling, lightly oiling the shaft bearings but taking care that oil is kept clear of the contacts. Adjust the contact points gap as described in **Section 3:2** prior to final setting when the distributor is installed, and check that the rotor shaft turns freely on the distributor shaft as permitted by the centrifugal mechanism.

3:5 Timing the ignition

Check that No. 1 piston is at TDC on the compression stroke and that the engine timing marks are correctly aligned as previously described. Install the distributor as described with the rotor pointing towards the stud for firing No. 1 cylinder, but do not fully tighten the clamp bolt to secure the distributor at this stage.

Connect a 12-volt test lamp in parallel with the contact breaker points. One lead will go to the terminal on the side of the distributor and one to earth. Switch on the ignition and ensure that the contact points are fully closed, turning the distributor body to ensure this. Now turn the distributor body very slowly until the lamp just lights up, which indicates that the points are beginning to open. Tighten the clamp bolt at this point and confirm the accuracy of the setting by turning the engine and checking that the test lamp lights up again exactly as the notch in the crankshaft pulley lines up with the appro-priate timing mark on the front cover. This procedure will ensure that the static advance setting of the distributor is correct. It is recommended that the centrifugal advance settings are then checked by a Fiat agent equipped with the necessary electronic equipment.

Stroboscopic timing:

If a stroboscopic timing lamp is available a more accurate setting can be obtained with the engine running at idling speed. Connect the lamp to No. 1 plug in accordance with the maker's instructions and add a spot of white paint to the two appropriate timing marks to make them more easily seen.

Start up the engine, run it at idling speed and aim the lamp at the timing marks. If the timing is correctly set, the marks will appear in line. If not, loosen the clamp and carefully rotate the distributor body as necessary to bring the marks into alignment.

The stroboscopic lamp can also be used on timing marks provided on the bellhousing and the flywheel as in **FIG 3:4.** Remove the rubber cover from the opening in the casing and aim the lamp at it while the engine is idling. The mark 0 on the flywheel should line up with the 10 deg. mark as shown or the 5 deg. mark on the 3P from 1976 and on all 1290 cc engines from 1977. Any necessary adjustment can be made as before.

3:6 Sparking plugs

Inspect and clean sparking plugs regularly. When removing sparking plugs, ensure that their recesses are clean and dry so that nothing can fall into the cylinders. Plug gaskets can be re-used, provided that they are not less than half their original thickness. Have sparking plugs cleaned on an abrasive-blasting machine and tested under pressure with electrode gaps correctly set at .6 to .7 mm (.024 to .028 inch). The electrodes should be filed until they are bright and parallel. The gaps must always be set by adjusting the earth electrode. **Do not try to bend the centre electrode.** Renew plugs at about 10,000 mile intervals, or before if badly worn.

Before refitting the plugs, clean the threads with a wire brush. Clean the threads in the cylinder head if the plugs cannot be screwed in by hand. Failing a tap for this purpose, use an old sparking plug with crosscuts down the threads. Plugs should be tightened with a proper plug spanner, through half a turn extra over finger tightness. Other types of spanner may slip off during tightening and crack the plug insulation.

Inspection of the deposits on the electrodes can be helpful when tuning. Normally, from mixed periods of high and low speed driving, the deposit should be powdery and range in colour from brown to greyish-tan. There will also be slight wear of the electrodes. Long periods of constant speed driving or low-speed city driving will give white or yellowish deposits. Dry, black fluffy deposits are due to incomplete combustion and indicate running with a rich mixture, excessive idling and, possibly, defective ignition. Overheated plugs have a white blistered look about the centre electrode and the side electrode may be badly eroded. This may be caused by poor cooling, incorrect ignition or sustained high speeds with heavy loads.

Black, wet deposits result from oil in the combustion chamber from worn pistons, rings, valve stems or guides. Sparking plugs which run hotter may alleviate the problem, but the cure is an engine overhaul.

Sparking plug leads:

Renew high-tension leads if they are defective in any way. Inspect for broken, swollen or deteriorated insulation which can be the cause of 'shorting', especially in wet weather conditions. Check the condition of the rubber covers on the terminal nuts and sparking plug connectors and renew them if they are split or perished. Thread new leads through the rubber covers and terminal nuts before refitting the lead end connectors.

3:7 Fault diagnosis

(a) Engine will not fire

1 Battery discharged
2 Contact breaker points dirty, pitted or maladjusted
3 Distributor cap dirty, cracked or 'tracking'
4 Brush inside distributor cap not touching rotor
5 Faulty cable or loose connection in low-tension circuit
6 Distributor rotor arm cracked or dirty
7 Faulty coil
8 Broken contact breaker spring
9 Contact points stuck open

(b) Engine misfires

1 Check 2, 3, 4 and 7 in (a)
2 Weak contact breaker spring
3 High-tension plug or coil leads cracked or perished
4 Sparking plug(s) loose
5 Sparking plug insulation cracked
6 Sparking plug gaps incorrectly set
7 Ignition timing too far advanced

(c) Poor acceleration

1 Ignition retarded
2 Centrifugal weights seized
3 Centrifugal springs weak, broken or disconnected
4 Distributor clamp loose
5 Excessive contact points gap
6 Worn plugs

NOTES

CHAPTER 4

THE COOLING SYSTEM

4:1 Description

The cooling system is pressurized and thermostatically controlled, using a corrugated fin type radiator. Water circulation is assisted by a centrifugal pump which is mounted at the front of the cylinder block. The four-blade cooling fan is driven by an electric motor mounted in the radiator shroud and is controlled by a thermo-switch mounted on the radiator.

The water pump is driven from the crankshaft pulley by a belt, this belt also driving the generator or alternator.

The water pump takes coolant from the bottom of the radiator and delivers it to the cylinder block from which it rises to the cylinder head. At normal operating temperatures the thermostat is open and the coolant returns to the top of the radiator. At lower temperatures, the thermostat is closed and the coolant bypasses the radiator and returns directly to the pump inlet. This provides a rapid warm-up.

4:2 Maintenance

The cooling system should be checked regularly for correct coolant level, when the engine is cool. Do not remove the filler cap from the radiator when the engine is hot, or coolant expansion may cause scalding as the pressure is released. To check the level, remove the cap and see if the coolant level is at the bottom of the filler neck. If not, add coolant as necessary. Check the level of coolant in the expansion chamber mounted on the front righthand wing valance and, if necessary, top up until the level is approximately 7 cm above the minimum mark.

The cooling system should periodically be drained, flushed to remove sediment and refilled. If antifreeze is in use, the coolant may be collected for re-use, but should be discarded after two winters. Check that the clips are tight on all hoses and that the radiator pressure cap is in good condition and that it seals effectively. Loss of coolant due to a leaking radiator cap can be a cause of engine overheating.

Draining:

Remove the front engine tray from beneath the car. Remove the radiator pressure cap and place the heater control lever on the dashboard to its lowest position. Open the radiator drain tap on the bottom right hand side of the radiator and the engine block drain tap situated on the generator side of the engine. Collect the coolant in a clean container if it is to be re-used.

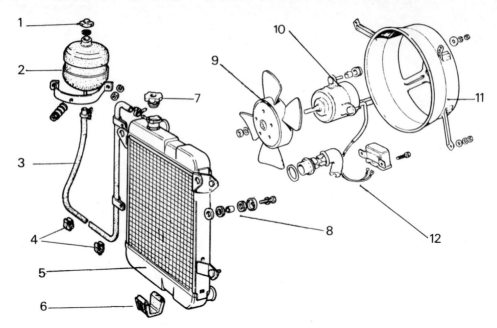

FIG 4:1   Radiator, expansion chamber and cooling fan

Key to Fig 4:1   1 Expansion chamber filler cap   2 Expansion chamber   3 Hose   4 Hose clips   5 Radiator
6 Radiator mounting   7 Radiator pressure cap   8 Mounting bolts   9 Cooling fan   10 Fan motor   11 Cooling
shroud   12 Thermo-switch assembly

FIG 4:2   The drive belt and pulleys, generator and alternator shown

Key to Fig 4:2   1 Generator pulley   2 Drive belt   3 Crankshaft pulley   4 Alternator pulley

Flushing:

Use a hose to run clean water in through the radiator filler until it runs clean at the drain plugs. Close the drain plugs, fill the system with water and run the engine long enough to warm up, so that the thermostat will open and allow complete circulation. Stop the engine and drain the system again before the sediment has had time to settle, taking care when handling the drain plugs as the water will now be hot. Repeat the flushing operation, close the drain plugs and refill the system to the levels mentioned previously.

4:3 Removing the radiator

Drain the cooling system as described in **Section 4:2** and disconnect the top and bottom hoses and the expansion chamber hose from the radiator. Refer to **FIG 4:1**. Disconnect the fan thermo-switch from the radiator and remove the air shroud assembly. Remove the radiator mounting bolts and lift out the radiator.

Refit in the reverse order of removal. On completion, refill the cooling system as described in **Section 4:2**.

4:4 Adjusting the drive belt

The drive belt tension is correct when it can be pressed down about 10 mm with firm hand pressure applied midway between the pulleys on the longest belt run, as shown in **FIG 4:3**. To adjust the belt tension, loosen the generator or alternator mounting and adjuster bolts, swing the unit in the required direction before re-tightening the mountings and rechecking the tension. The belt can be removed by slackening the bolts and moving the generator or alternator inwards until the belt can be removed over the pulleys.

A tight drive belt will cause undue wear on the pulleys and component bearings, a slack belt will cause slip and, possibly, engine overheating and reduced generator or alternator output.

4:5 The water pump

Removal:

Refer to **FIG 4:4**. Drain the cooling system and disconnect the top and bottom hoses from the water pump. Remove the radiator air shroud and remove the drive belt, as described previously. Disconnect the heater hoses. Slacken the generator mounting bolts and remove the upper bracket from the pump. Remove the water pump from the engine block, collecting the mounting gasket.

Refitting:

This is a reversal of the removal procedure, using a new mounting gasket. Refill the cooling system on completion, as described previously.

Dismantling:

Remove the cover from the housing complete with pulley, shaft and impeller. Remove the pulley in a press using tool set A.40040. Remove the impeller using extractor A.40026. Unscrew the stop screw and press out the drive shaft and bearings. Slide off the two bearings, spacer, snap ring shroud and snap ring from the shaft. Drift the seal out of the cover.

Thoroughly clean all parts and inspect them for wear or damage. Renew all faulty parts, then reassemble the pump in the reverse order of dismantling noting the following points.

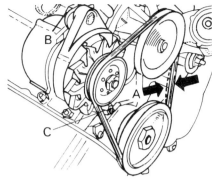

FIG 4:3 Drive belt tensioning

Key to Fig 4:3   **A** Belt deflection   **B** Adjusting nut
C Alternator mounting nut

Renew the two internal grommets in the pump cover.

When pressing on the impeller to the point where it contacts the seal the impeller is placed on the seating in tool A.60373/1 distance piece A.60373/2 is fitted to the top end of the shaft and the pump cover and shaft is pressed into the impeller until the cover contacts the tool A.60373/1. Tighten the fixture screw A.60373/3 until a clearance is obtained of 2 to 3 mm between the cover and tool A.60373/1.

Ensure that there is a clearance of 0.8 to 1.3 mm between the impeller and the pump housing when assembly is complete.

4:6 The thermostat

The thermostat is located in a housing mounted on the engine block.

Removal:

Drain sufficient coolant to bring the level below that of the thermostat assembly. Refer to **FIG 4:4**. Remove the spare wheel from the engine compartment.

Disconnect the four hoses from the thermostat housing and then unscrew the mounting bolts and lift away the complete assembly.

Unscrew the housing cover bolts and withdraw the thermostat and seal.

Refitting:

This is a reversal of the removal procedure, using new gaskets.

Testing:

Clean the thermostat and immerse it in a container of cold water together with a zero to 100°C thermometer. Heat the water, keeping it stirred, and check that the valve opens at approximately 82°C and is fully open at approximately 95°C. The valve should close tightly when the thermostat is removed from the hot water and placed in cold water. If the thermostat operates correctly it may be refitted, but if not it must be renewed.

4:7 The cooling fan

The cooling fan is electrically operated and switched on and off, according to engine temperature, by a thermo-switch attached to the radiator. The cut-in temperature is 94°C to 98°C and the cut-out temperature is 1°C less than

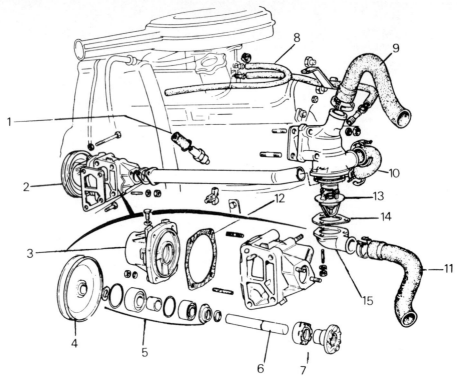

FIG 4:4   Water pump, thermostat and water hoses

Key to Fig 4:4   1 Temperature sender unit   2 Water pump assembly   3 Pump housing   4 Pump pulley   5 Pump bearing assembly   6 Pump shaft   7 Pump impeller assembly   8 Heater and carburetter heater hoses   9 Top radiator hose 10 Pump to thermostat hose   11 Bottom radiator hose   12 Pump gasket   13 Thermostat   14 Thermostat gasket 15 Thermostat housing

the cut-in setting. If the fan operates with the engine cold, the switch is faulty or there is a short-circuit in the fan wiring. If the fan does not operate at all, check the fuse, then check that the motor is in order by connecting jumper leads from the battery to the motor terminals. If the motor is in order, check the wiring to the motor, thermo-switch or relay. If the wiring and connections are in order, suspect a faulty thermo-switch or relay.

4:8 Frost precautions

If antifreeze is to be used, the system should first be drained and flushed as described in **Section 4:2** and all hoses checked for tightness. Ethylene-glycol type anti-freeze or, preferably, Fiat special antifreeze should be added in the proportions recommended by the manu-facturer, to give protection from freezing in the lowest temperatures at which the car is to be operated. After the second winter, drain and flush the system and refill with fresh solution. When antifreeze is in use, a suitable strength antifreeze solution should be used for topping up, when necessary. If plain water only is used for topping up purposes, the antifreeze will be diluted, perhaps to the stage where it no longer affords protection from freezing.

4:9 Fault diagnosis

(a) Internal water leakage

1 Cracked cylinder wall
2 Loose cylinder head bolts

3 Cracked cylinder head
4 Faulty head gasket

(b) Poor circulation

1 Radiator blocked
2 Engine water passages restricted
3 Low coolant level
4 Slack pump drive belt
5 Defective thermostat
6 Perished or collapsed radiator hoses

(c) Corrosion

1 Impurities in the coolant
2 Infrequent draining and flushing

(d) Overheating

1 Check (b)
2 Sludge in crankcase
3 Faulty ignition timing
4 Low oil level in engine sump
5 Tight engine
6 Choke exhaust system
7 Binding brakes
8 Slipping clutch
9 Incorrect valve timing
10 Retarded ignition
11 Mixture too weak
12 Faulty fan motor or switch

CHAPTER 5

THE CLUTCH

5 : 1 Description

The clutch is a single dry plate unit of diaphragm spring type. The main components are the driven plate, pressure plate assembly and release bearing.

The driven plate consists of a resilient steel disc attached to a hub which slides on the splined clutch shaft. The friction linings are riveted to both sides of the disc.

The pressure plate assembly consists of the pressure plate, diaphragm spring and housing, the assembly being bolted to the engine flywheel. The release bearing is a ballbearing of special construction with an elongated ring that presses directly against the diaphragm spring when the clutch pedal is operated. The bearing is mounted on a carrier and operated from a fork and pivot rod journalled in the clutch housing.

The clutch pedal movement is transmitted to the release bearing by a sheathed steel cable attached to the clutch release lever.

When the clutch is fully engaged, the driven plate is nipped between the pressure plate and the engine fly-wheel and transmits torque to the gearbox through the splined input shaft. When the clutch pedal is depressed, the pressure plate is withdrawn from the driven plate by force transmitted through the cable and the driven plate ceases to transmit torque to the gearbox.

5 : 2 Adjusting the clutch

Clutch adjustment should be checked regularly, as normal wear of the driven plate linings will alter the adjustment in service. If the cable is adjusted with insufficient free play, the cable will be tight and tend to prevent the clutch from engaging properly, causing slip and rapid clutch plate wear. If the cable has too much free play, the clutch will not release properly, causing drag and consequent poor gearchange qualities and difficulty in engaging gears from rest.

The clutch adjustment point at the end of the operating cable are shown in **FIG 5 : 1**. **FIG 5 : 2** shows the effect of cable adjustment at both the release bearing and the clutch pedal.

Check the amount of free play at the clutch pedal, operating the pedal by hand. If play is not as shown in the illustration, slacken the locknut 1 and adjust the nut 2 until the correct free play is obtained, then retighten the locknut and recheck the adjustment. Lubricate the cable ball at point **c** in **FIG 5 : 2**. This adjustment procedure will set the clutch internal clearances to the figures shown.

5 : 3 Removing and dismantling clutch

Refer to **Chapter 6** and remove the gearbox. Mark the position of the clutch cover relative to the engine flywheel,

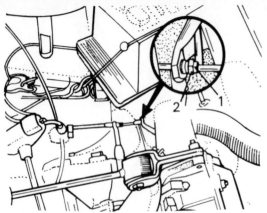

FIG 5:1   Clutch cable locknut 1 and adjusting nut 2

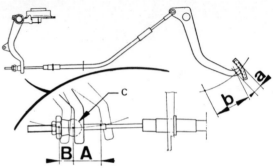

FIG 5:2   Clutch adjustment details

Key to Fig 5:2   a 25 mm pedal free play   **b** 102 mm pedal travel during clutch release   **A** 25 mm release lever travel during clutch release   **B** 12.5 mm movement of throwout lever with worn down driven plate linings   **C** Cable to release lever lubrication point

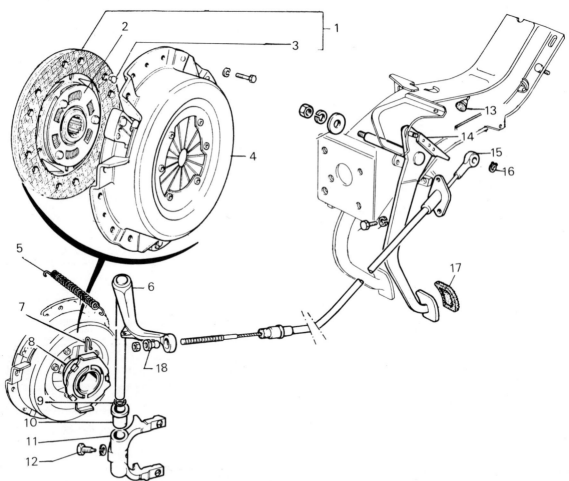

FIG 5:3   Clutch and release mechanism, pedal and cable assembly

Key to Fig 5:3   1 Clutch assembly   2 Driven plate   3 Rivet   4 Pressure plate   5 Return spring   6 Release lever   7 Clip   8 Release bearing and carrier   9 Washer   10 Bush   11 Release bearing fork   12 Lockscrew   13 Pedal stop   14 Pedal   15 Clevis   16 Circlip   17 Pedal rubber   18 Cable adjuster

using paint or light punch marks, so that the unit can be refitted in its original position and thus preserve the balance of the assembly. Lock the flywheel against rotation by suitable means, then loosen the six clutch cover fixing screws alternately and evenly to prevent distortion until the spring pressure is released. Remove the screws and disengage the clutch mechanism. Remove the clutch assembly from the flywheel, disengaging the three centring dowels. Take care not to allow grease or oil onto the driven plate linings.

Thoroughly clean all parts in a suitable solvent, with the exception of the driven plate linings and the release bearing. The release bearing must not be cleaned in solvents as this would wash the internal lubricant from the bearing.

The clutch cover, spring and pressure plate assembly is an integral unit and must not be dismantled. If any part is defective the assembly must be renewed complete.

Inspect the surface of the flywheel where the driven plate makes contact. Small cracks on the surface are unimportant, but if there are any deep scratches, the flywheel should be machined smooth or renewed. Check the pressure plate for scoring or damage and that the operating surface is flat and true. Check the diaphragm spring for cracks or other damage and the release bearing for roughness when it is pressed and turned by hand. Any parts which are worn or damaged must be renewed.

Check the driven plate for loose rivets and broken or very loose torsional springs. The friction linings should be well proud of the rivets and have a light colour, with a polished glaze through which the grain of the material is clearly visible. A dark, glazed deposit indicates oil on the facings and, as this condition cannot be rectified, a new or relined plate will be required. Any sign of oil in the clutch should be investigated as to the cause, and rectified to prevent recurrence of the problem. Check the disc for runout at the outer circumference, preferably using a dial gauge. Maximum permissible runout is .20 mm, any figure in excess of this being liable to cause clutch judder or snatch in operation, plus rapid wear of the components. Attempts to rectify a warped driven plate are not likely to be successful and a new unit should be obtained.

It is not recommended that owners attempt to reline the clutch driven plate themselves, as the linings must be riveted and trued on the disc and the whole checked under a press. For this reason, the driven plate should be relined at a service station or an exchange unit obtained and fitted. Check the driven plate hub for a smooth, sliding fit on the splined shaft, removing any burrs on the shaft or in the hub.

5:4 Assembling and refitting clutch

Place the driven disc in position, with the hub offset towards the gearbox side. Place the clutch pressure plate assembly in position, aligning the marks made previously and the centring dowels in their respective holes. Centre the disc on the engine flywheel by inserting too. A.70210 through the assembly and into the pilot bearing in the flywheel, as shown in **FIG 5:5**. With the tool in position, fit the clutch assembly retaining screws and tighten them alternately and evenly. Remove the aligning tool and refit the gearbox in the manner described in **Chapter 6**. Adjust the cable as described in **Section 5:2**.

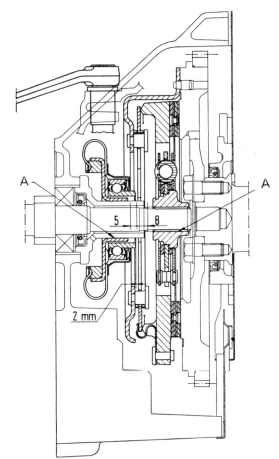

FIG 5:4 Clutch assembly cross-section

Key to Fig 5:4   **2 mm** Clearance at release bearing when the control cable adjustment is correct   **5 mm** Maximum acceptable movement with worn driven plate linings **8 mm** Declutching travel   **A** Lubrication points to be thinly smeared with FIAT KG 15 grease

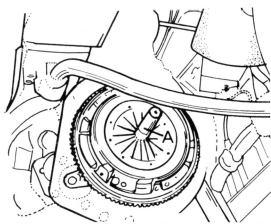

FIG 5:5 Clutch driven plate alignment with special tool

5:5 Clutch cable renewal

If the clutch cable is damaged or stretched, it can be renewed by removing the cable connection at the pedal clevis and removing the lock and adjusting nuts at the release lever connection. Fit the new cable in the reverse order, adjusting the pedal free play, on completion, as described in **Section 5:2**.

5:6 Fault diagnosis

(a) Drag or spin

1 Oil or grease on driven plate linings
2 Control cable binding
3 Distorted driven plate
4 Warped or damaged pressure plate
5 Broken driven plate linings
6 Excessive clutch free play

(b) Fierceness or snatch

1 Check 1, 2, 3 and 4 in (a)
2 Worn driven plate linings

(c) Slip

1 Check 1 in (a) and 2 in (b)
2 Weak diaphragm spring
3 Seized control cable
4 Insufficient clutch pedal free play

(d) Judder

1 Check 1, 3 and 4 in (a)
2 Contact area of friction linings unevenly worn
3 Bent or worn splined shaft
4 Badly worn splines in driven plate hub
5 Faulty engine or gearbox mountings

(e) Tick or knock

1 Badly worn driven plate hub splines
2 Worn release bearing
3 Bent or worn splined shaft
4 Loose flywheel

CHAPTER 6

THE TRANSMISSION

6:1 Description

A fourspeed all synchromesh gearbox is fitted, gear operation being from the floor mounted gearlever. The gearbox assembly is fitted in line with the engine and incorporates the clutch housing, the differential unit and drive shaft being mounted below the gearbox as shown in **FIG 6:1**. Sections through the transmission components are shown in **FIG 6:2**.

Flexible ring type synchromesh units are fitted and a helical tooth pinion final drive is used. Final drive ratios are given in **Technical Data**. The drive is transmitted to the front wheels by drive shafts fitted with constant velocity joints at both wheel hubs and differential, these joints accommodating both steering and suspension movements.

6:2 Routine maintenance

Every 5000 kilometres, or whenever underbody inspections are carried out, check the condition of the transmission drive shaft rubber boots. If the boots are damaged in any way, renew them. Every 30,000 kilometres, check the lubrication of the wheel hub constant velocity joints and add Fiat MRM2 grease if necessary.

Every 10,000 kilometres, check the gearbox oil level and top up if necessary with Fiat ZC.90 oil. The gearbox oil level should be maintained at the lower edge of the combined filler and level hole shown at **A** in **FIG 6:3**. Every 30,000 kilometres the oil should be drained from the gearbox when the unit is hot, by removing plug **B**. On completion, refit the drain plug and refill to the level of plug **A** with the correct oil. The car should be standing on level ground when oil level checks are made.

6:3 Front half axles

Removal:

To disconnect the transmission shafts for power unit removal proceed as follows:

With the vehicle on supports take off the lefthand wheel and disconnect the steering arm using ball joint remover A.47044.

Detach the shock absorber from the steering swivel by removing the screws and nuts.

Unscrew the constant speed joint nuts from both hubs.

Wire the shafts to the differential to prevent disturbance of the inner seats. **FIG 6:4** shows a section through the unit.

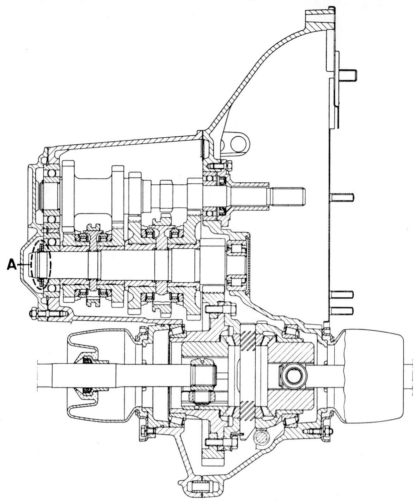

FIG 6:1   The transmission and final drive

Refitting:

This is a reversal of the removal procedure. On completion check the front wheel geometry as described in **Chapters 7** and **9**.

6:4   Transmission shafts

Removal:

Drain the gearbox oil as described in **Section 6:2**. Remove the nuts and screws fixing the retaining flanges of the shaft protectors to the gearbox. **FIG 6:5** shows the components of the transmission shaft assemblies.

Remove the outer clamps holding the protectors onto their constant velocity joints and push back the protectors to uncover the joints. Thoroughly clean the joint assemblies.

Open the circlip using circlip pliers as shown in **FIG 6:6**, then withdraw the shaft ends from the constant velocity joint splines. Lock the wheel until the shafts are clear of the constant velocity joints. Disengage the shafts from the gearbox sides, withdrawing them outwards.

Refitting:

Refitting is a reversal of the removal procedure, noting the following points. Fit the gearbox end of the shaft with the wheel on full lock, then straighten the wheel and fit the other end. Engage the shaft in the constant velocity joint as shown in **FIG 6:7**. Make sure that the retainer is well positioned in the groove by pushing the shaft inwards then pulling it outwards, repeating this several times. Pack the constant velocity joint with the correct grade of grease. Position the rubber protector retaining flanges properly, then replace the outer retaining rings to secure the protectors.

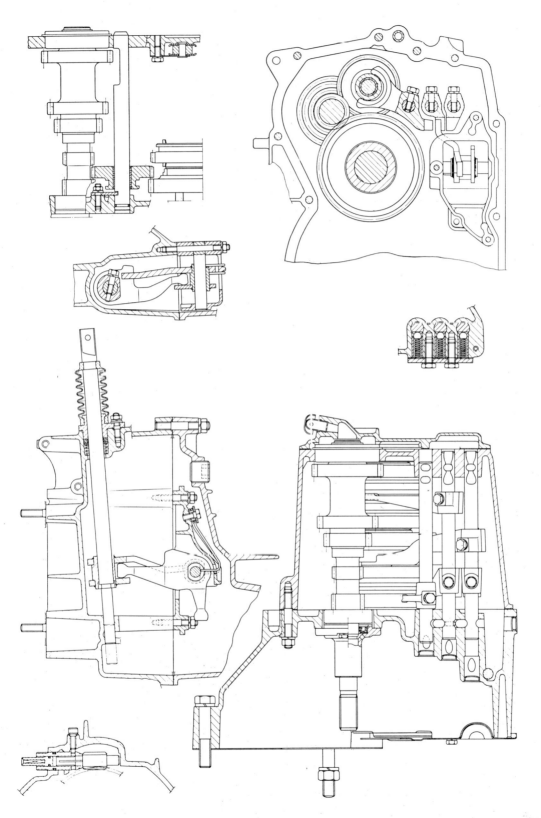

FIG 6:2 Transmission sections

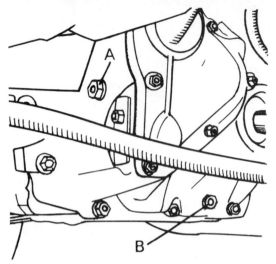

FIG 6:3   The gearbox oil filler (A) and drain plugs (B)

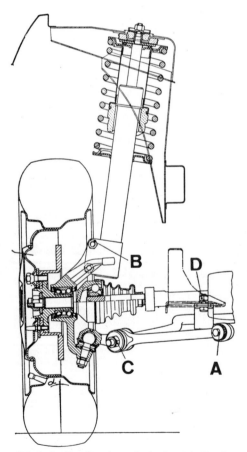

FIG 6:4   Section through the front half axle

6:5 Gearbox removal and refitting
Removal:

Raise the front of the car and safely support it on floor stands. Remove the transmission shafts and the starter motor. Remove the centre crossmember from beneath the car and support the weight of the engine with a jack, as shown in **FIG 6:8.** Remove the engine flywheel lateral cover. Disconnect the gearchange linkage and the speedometer drive from the gearbox. Remove the clutch operating cable at the gearbox end, as described in **Chapter 5.** Unscrew the clutch housing surround. Supporting the gearbox during the operation, slide the gearbox away from the engine and remove it, taking care not to allow the weight of the gearbox to rest on the input shaft while the shaft is in the clutch unit. Clutch damage can easily occur if the driven plate is twisted by the gearbox input shaft.

Refitting:

This is a reversal of the removal procedure, again taking care not to damage the clutch unit with the gearbox input shaft. If the clutch unit has been disturbed, realignment must be carried out as described in **Chapter 5.** Check the clutch adjustment and the gearbox oil level on completion.

6:6 Gearbox dismantling

FIGS 6:9, 6:10 and **6:11** show the components of the gearbox and gearchange assemblies.

Drain the oil from the gearbox. Mount the gearbox in a vice, holding it by the rear lower reinforcement. Remove the drive plate at the differential end. Remove the retaining nuts from the two half casings, then split the casings. Remove the differential and crownwheel assembly.

Remove the gearbox cover at the support end. Position tool A.70226 (see **FIG 6:12**) and compress the Belleville washers situated under the snap ring at the end of the secondary shaft. Screw in the centre part of the tool until the snap ring is free in its groove. Open the end of the snap ring with special pliers and, at the same time, unscrew tool A.70226 to progressively release the Belleville washers. These washers are shown at **A** in **FIG 6:1.** Remove the special tools.

Remove the primary shaft snap ring. Remove the pointed retaining screw of the third- and fourth-speed fork and the reversing light contact support. Remove the three springs and three locking balls of the selector fork shafts, noting that the reverse gear spring is coloured red.

Expel the primary and secondary shafts, using a bronze drift through the gearbox rear end. The rear bearings are not removed. Recover the selector fork shaft plungers from the casing. Remove the gearchange control by releasing the snap ring at the end of the shaft. Dismantle the secondary shaft.

Clean all parts thoroughly and examine the condition of the gears, synchromesh assemblies and selector mechanisms. Renew any part found worn or damaged.

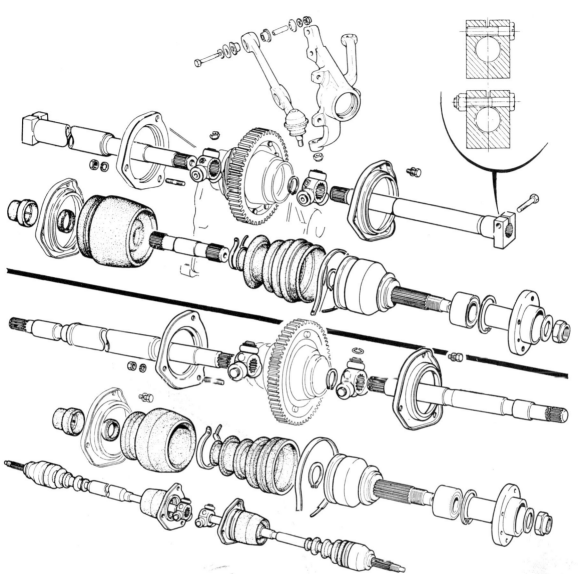

FIG 6:5   Transmission shaft assemblies

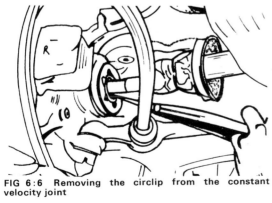

FIG 6:6   Removing the circlip from the constant velocity joint

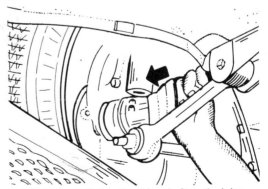

FIG 6:7   Refitting the drive shaft to the joint

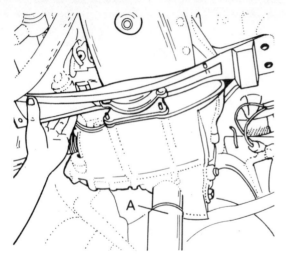

FIG 6:8 Removing the centre crossmember and supporting the engine with a jack shown at A

Synchromesh operation:

2nd, 3rd and 4th gear engagement:

The sliding sleeve is internally toothed to engage the synchronizer ring external teeth, which is brazed onto the inside face of the pinion mounted free on the output shaft. In this manner, the pinion is locked in position on the driving hub.

The synchronizer ring 2 ensures the progressive equalization of the rotational speeds as the sleeve moves into position. As soon as ring 2 comes into contact with the sliding sleeve, the ring is driven or stopped, whichever

is the case, and in consequence one of its ends butts onto the locking plate. This starts a circling motion so that synchronization occurs rapidly.

To increase the friction of the synchronizer ring on the slider, two driving springs are fitted, one working during deceleration, the other during acceleration. In effect, the spring is compressed between the locking plate and the stop. This causes the spring to be compressed against the synchronizer ring.

The synchronizing action of the ring under its own tension is thus progressively increased by the radial pressure of the spring. This action continues until the speed difference between the slider and the driven pinion is fully equalized. At this moment, the spring action ceases and the synchronizer ring locks.

It is therefore possible for the slider to move with very little applied effort until a smooth gear engagement takes place. At that moment, the synchronizer ring expands in a circular groove machined in the protruding sections of the internal teeth of the slider and the chosen gear is locked in position.

1st gear engagement:

In order to reduce to a minimum the effort required to engage first gear when the vehicle is either moving or at rest, a single driving spring has been fitted, which only comes into operation when changing down from second to first gear. Furthermore, locking plate 3 is fitted with an inside lug which engages a slot in the pinion synchronizing crown. When starting, with the engine turning slowly, it is sufficient to damp out the inertia of the clutch disc.

The end of the synchronizer spring contacts the locking plate and the internal lug butts against the synchronizer crown. The particular shape of the lug

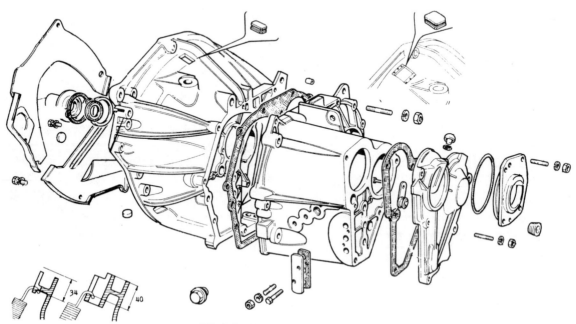

FIG 6:9 Gearbox case components

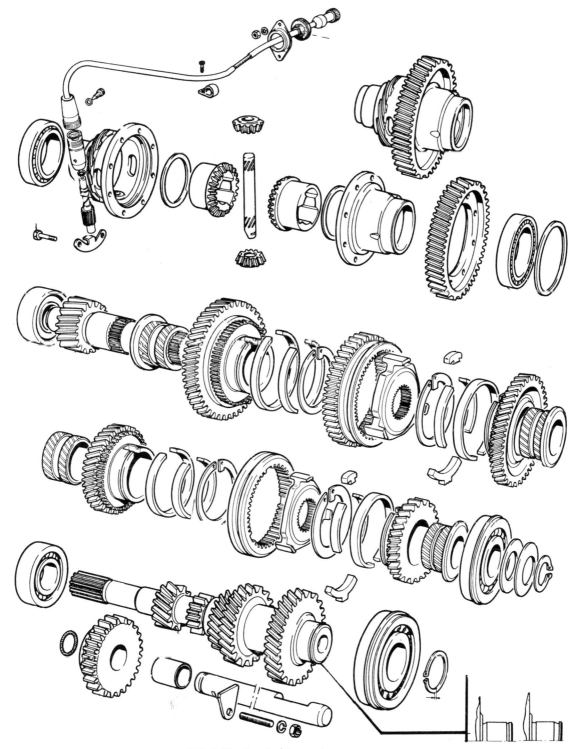

FIG 6:10   Gearbox internal components

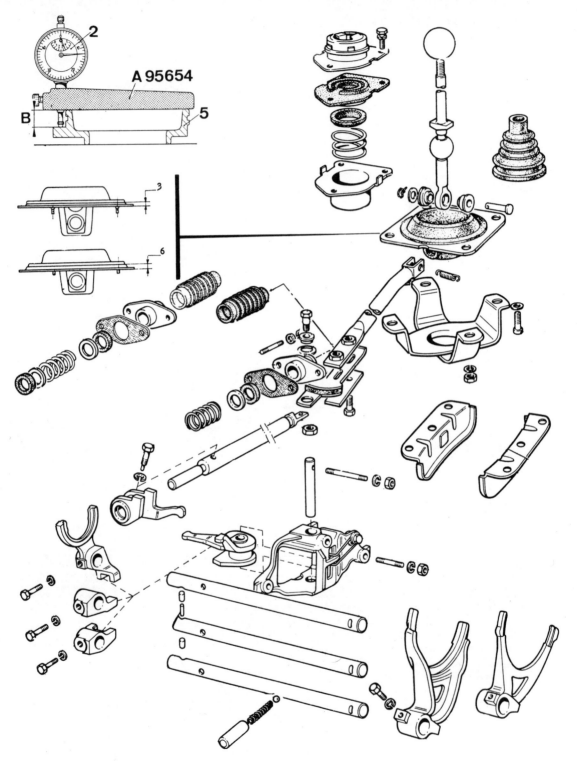

FIG 6:11   Gearchange linkage components

causes the locking plate to lift up, thus increasing the radial thrust of the spring. When changing down from second to first gear, synchronization takes place in the same manner as for a downchange from fourth to third gear.

Checking synchromesh units:

The synchronizer ring friction surface is moybdenum coated. If this surface is rough, it will be necessary to renew the ring. The external diameter of a new spring when fitted is 76.31 ± .2 for first and second gears and 66.22 ± .2 mm for third and fourth gears. After a certain period of use, due to the settling of the ring caused by friction against the pinion crown and the slider, the diameter is increased slightly. This increase in diameter permits perfectly smooth gearchanging.

When reassembling the gearbox, check that the synchronizer spring fits without play in its seat on the pinion, that the internal teeth on the sliding sleeve are free from wear or burrs and that any new springs fitted are of the specified diameter.

Dismantling and reassembling synchromesh units:

Remove the stop ring, then remove the drive springs and locking plates.

Refit the springs and plates and replace the stop ring, this being facilitated by the use of tool A.70100/1/2, as shown in **FIG 6 : 14**.

6.7 Gearbox reassembly

Fit the double row ballbearings on the primary shaft inner end. Fit the inner ring of the roller bearing on the inner end of the secondary shaft. Working from the outer end, fit the following parts on the secondary shaft, in the order stated. Fourth-speed ring and fourth-speed pinion, the hub and slider for the third- and fourth-speed pinion, the third-speed pinion with its ring, the first- and second-speed slider and hub and the first-speed pinion with its ring.

Note that the synchronizer hub grooves must be opposite each other and that the synchronizer cones must be fitted with the small diameter ends facing each other.

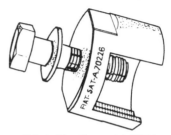

FIG 6 : 12   Fiat tool A.70226

Position the secondary shaft complete, position the primary shaft and engage the pinion teeth. Fit at the same time the selector shafts and forks, the locking tenons and the reverse gear on the dummy shaft of the special tool obtainable for the purpose. Engage the gearbox casing onto this assembly.

Fit the ballbearings on the ends of the primary and secondary shafts. The primary shaft bearing is held in position by two Belleville washers and a retainer ring. Place the washers, facing each other, and the retainer ring on the shaft, then position the compressor tool A.70226. Compress the washers by screwing in the centre part of the tool and engage the retainer in its groove. Remove the special tools. Complete the fitting of the selector mechanism and gearchange assembly.

Differential unit:

Place the right hand planetary wheel together with its thrust washer in the differential casing. These washers are available in .85, .90, 1.00, 1.05, 1.10 and 1.15 mm thicknesses. Place in position the satellites and their shaft, with the bevel on the shaft facing the righthand planetary wheel. Position the lefthand planetary wheel and its thrust washer in the crownwheel. Assemble the differential casing and the crownwheel, ensuring that the reference marks coincide. Fit the sheet metal locking plates on the satellite shaft and tighten the nuts to 8 mdaN. Grease all parts and check that rotational torque is between 3 and 5 mdaN with the differential casing free and one of the

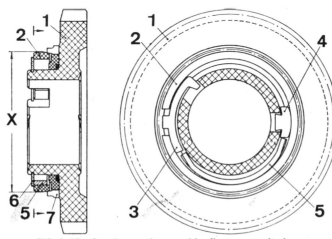

FIG 6 : 13   Synchromesh assembly, first gear unit shown

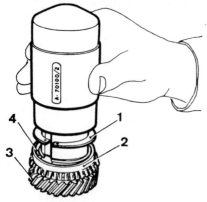

FIG 6:14 Reassembling a synchromesh unit

planetaries locked. If the torque is excessive, fit thinner thrust washers, if the torque is insufficient, fit thicker washers.

Using a suitable piece of tubing placed against the inner bearing ring, refit the ballbearings on the differential housing and the crownwheel. Fit the secondary shaft roller bearing outer ring in the clutch housing. Place the differential on the gearbox housing, with the lipped sealing ring in between. Reassemble the casing, gearbox and clutch housing and tighten the nuts to 2.5 mdaN.

Note that, if overheating of the gearbox oil has caused the outer ring of the secondary shaft bearing to move in its seat, Loctite can be used to cure the trouble.

Differential bearing setting:

After fitting and adjusting the differential casing sealing cover, the differential bearings must have a preload of .06 to .10 mm. The correct preload is obtained by means

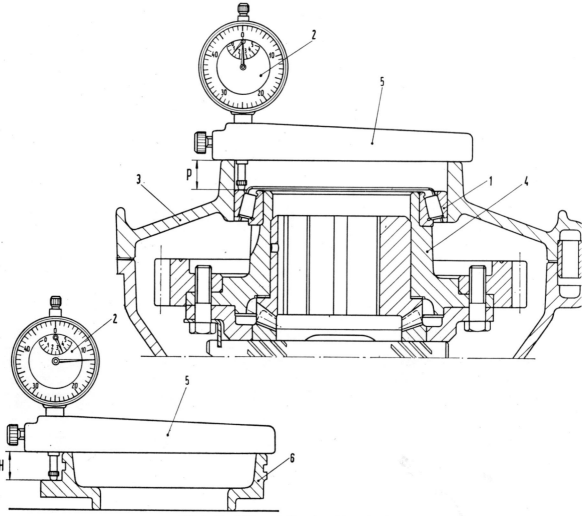

FIG 6:15 Differential bearing shim selection

Key to Fig 6:15 1 Roller bearing   2 Dial indicator   3 Transmission case   4 Differential case   5 Tool A.95654
6 Sealing cover   **P** Distance between bearing cup (1) and sealing cover mounting face   **H** Height of sealing cover

of adjusting shims fitted between the righthand bearing outer ring and the cover. The total thickness of washers is calculated as follows, while exerting an axial load of about 350 kg on the outer ring of the bearing.

Refer to **FIG 6:15**. Before taking a reading of **P**, settle the bearings by applying increasing axial load until a give-in of .04 mm is shown on the dial indicator. Measure the distance **P**, then measure the flange distance **H**. Thickness of shims required is calculated thus:

$$S = P - H + .08 \text{ mm.}$$

6:8 Fault diagnosis

(a) Jumping out of gear

1 Excessively worn selector shafts
2 Worn synchromesh assemblies
3 Loose or worn selector fork

(b) Noisy transmission

1 Insufficient oil
2 Bearings worn or damaged
3 Worn drive shaft joints
4 Worn synchromesh units

(c) Difficulty in engaging gear

1 Incorrect clutch adjustment
2 Worn synchromesh assemblies
3 Worn selector shafts or forks

(d) Oil leaks

1 Damaged joint washers or gaskets
2 Worn or damaged oil seals
3 Faulty joint faces on gearbox case components

NOTES

CHAPTER 7

FRONT SUSPENSION AND HUBS

7:1 Description

The independent front wheel suspension is by means of helically coiled springs controlled by double-acting hydraulic telescopic dampers. The damper units also act as pivots for the front wheel stub axle assemblies, to accommodate steering movement. The suspension springs are fitted co-axially to the damper struts between two pressed steel support cups. A Teflon plastic bush is interposed between the top support cup and the suspension strut support to facilitate free rotation during steering movement. The elastic strut guides are also Teflon coated to reduce friction.

The front wheel hubs rotate on the stub axle assemblies, being carried on a single, wide ballbearing unit fitted at each stub axle and retained by a circlip.

The front wheel stub axle assembly is located at the upper point by the damper unit attachment and at the lower point by a short control arm and the anti-roll bar. The anti-roll bar, mounted on rubber bushings to the car body, acts as a control arm for the front suspension in addition to providing lateral stability to the car during cornering or while driving over rough surfaces. The anti-roll bar is connected to the lower control arm at each side of the car, these attachment points being provided with means for setting the front wheel castor angle.

Ball joints are used at the control arm to stub axle connecting to accommodate movement during suspension travel. All joints and pivots in the front suspension are lubricated for life, no maintenance being required.

7:2 Ball joints

The front suspension ball joints should be inspected every 5000 kilometres or whenever inspection of the underbody is carried out. Examine the ball joint rubber caps for splits, holes or other damage and renew them if not in perfect condition. The new caps must be filled with Fiat MR.3 grease prior to installation. At the same time, check the ball joints for excessive play. If evidence of looseness exists, the control arm in question must be renewed, no servicing being possible as they are sealed assemblies.

7:3 Wheel hubs

Removal:

Raise the front of the car and safely support it on floor stands. Remove the road wheel. Remove the hub nut. Detach the front brake caliper from the steering knuckle assembly. Without detaching the brake hose, withdraw the caliper assembly from the brake disc and hang the

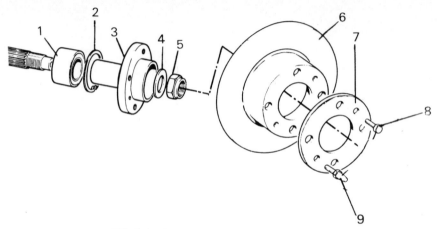

FIG 7:1 Front wheel hub and bearing details

Key to Fig 7:1   1 Wheel bearing   2 Circlip (or nut from 1972)   3 Wheel hub   4 Nut collar   5 Hub nut   6 Brake disc
7 Hub flange   8 Bolt   9 Locating stud

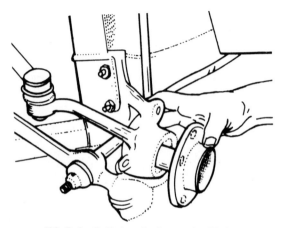

FIG 7:2   Refitting the front wheel hub

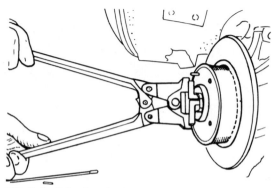

FIG 7:3   Crimping the hub nut collar with the special tool

caliper on the front suspension so that the hose is not strained, using a wire hook or similar means. Remove the brake disc from the hub, undo the bolts and nuts and disengage the steering knuckle from the suspension strut. Disconnect the steering tie rod at the ball joint using ball joint remover A.47044. Disconnect the control arm at the ball joint in the same manner. Pull the knuckle and hub from the shaft, then withdraw the hub from the steering knuckle.

Wheel bearing renewal:

Refer to **FIG 7:1**. Remove the retaining circlip or nut 2 and extract the wheel bearing 1. Carefully clean the bearing housing in the knuckle. Coat the bearing housing firstly with Locquic Aktivator, then with sealing Loctite. Fit the new bearing into the housing and refit the retaining circlip. Where a ring nut is fitted use adaptor A.57123 and a torque wrench and tighten the nut to 43.5 lb ft and stake the nut in position, always renew the ring nut if removed.

Refitting:

Refit the hub assembly by hand, as shown in **FIG 7:2**. If difficulty is experienced in fitting, use a threaded rod to facilitate the operation. Reconnect the drive shaft to the wheel hub. Refit the brake disc to the hub. Refit the brake caliper to the steering knuckle, tightening the mounting screws to a torque of 36 lb ft. Tighten the wheel hub nut to a torque of 101 lb ft (116 lb ft from 1973 models), then crimp the nut collar to lock the nut, preferably using the special tool as shown in **FIG 7:3**. Tighten ball joint nuts to 25.5 lb ft.

7:4 Suspension units

Removal:

FIG 7:4 shows the upper and lower suspension strut mounting points. Slacken the front damper fixing point on the wheel arch (see **FIG 7:5**). Raise the front of the car and safely support it on floor stands, then remove the front wheel. Remove the screws and nuts securing the strut unit to the steering knuckle, then remove the damper and spring assembly from the car.

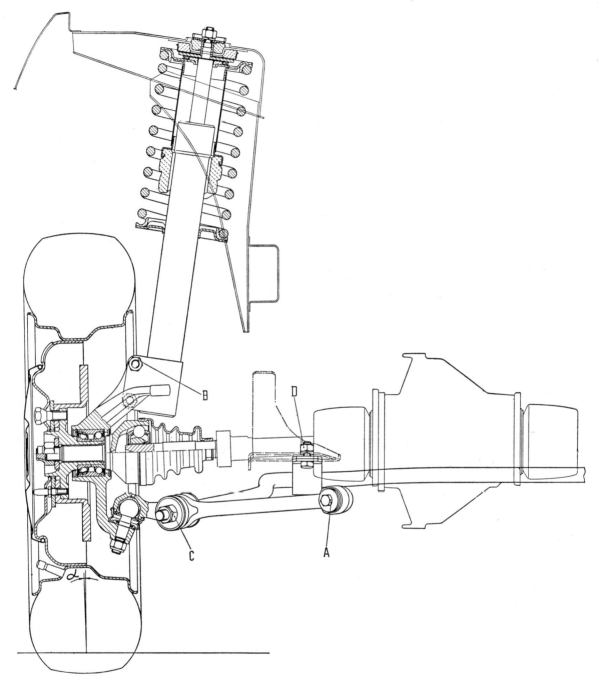

FIG 7:4 Front suspension layout (lefthand side)

Key to Fig 7:4   A Control arm to body mounting   **B** Suspension strut to steering knuckle screws and nuts   **C** Anti-roll bar to control arm nut   **D** Anti-roll bar to body screws and nuts

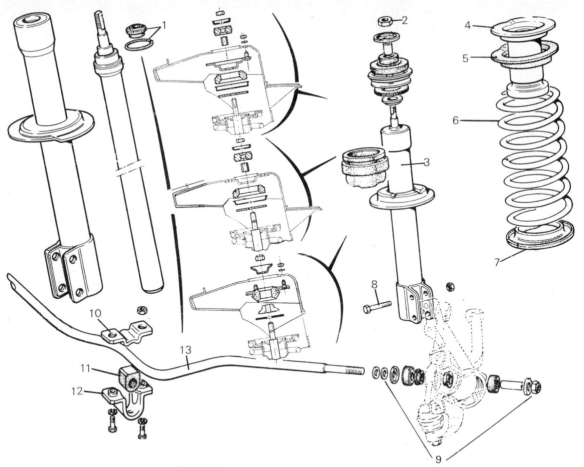

FIG 7:5 Damper, spring and anti-roll bar details

Key to Fig 7:5   1 Rubber mountings   2 Upper damper attaching nut   3 Suspension strut   4 Spring mounting
5 Upper spring seat   6 Coil spring   7 Lower spring seat   8 Lower mounting screw   9 Anti-roll bar to control arm mounting
10 Upper bracket   11 Rubber bush   12 Lower bracket   13 Anti-roll bar

Refitting:

This is a reversal of the removal procedure. Tighten the damper upper mounting nut to 18 lb ft or adaptor nuts to 7 lb ft and the lower strut attaching screws to 43 lb ft. On completion, the front suspension geometry must be checked as described in **Section 7:6**. Final tightening of the components should be carried out with the car loaded as described in **Section 7:6**.

Spring removal:

With the suspension strut assembly removed from the car, compress the coil spring with a suitably sturdy compressor, remembering that personal injury could result if the spring were to slip. Remove the spring mountings and remove the spring from the strut assembly. Refit the spring in the reverse order of removal. **FIG 7:5** shows spring and damper details.

7:5 Anti-roll bar

Removal:

Raise and safely support the front of the car (see **FIG 7:5**). Remove the anti-roll bar to car body brackets. Disconnect the anti-roll bar from the control arms on both sides of the car, collecting the shims and noting their positions for correct refitting.

Refitting:

This is a reversal of the removal instructions, noting the instructions in **Section 7:6** when tightening the fixings. On completion, the suspension geometry must be checked as described in **Section 7:6**.

7:6 Steering geometry

Every 10,000 kilometres as part of normal servicing, whenever suspension components have been dismantled,

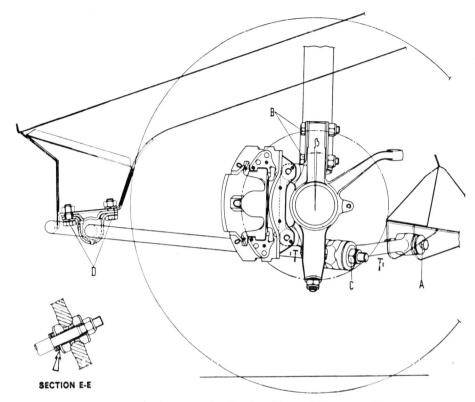

SECTION E-E

FIG 7:6   Castor angle adjusting shim position arrowed

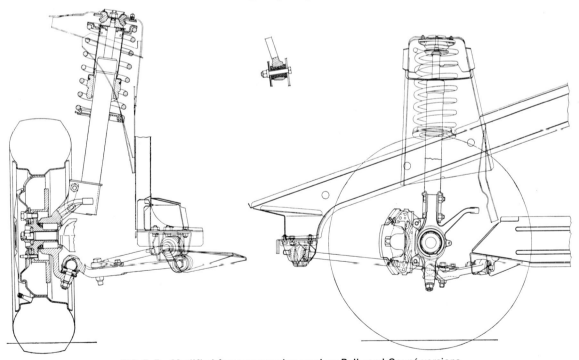

FIG 7:7   Modified front suspension used on Rally and Coupé versions

or at any time when uneven tyre wear has been noted, the front suspension castor and camber angles should be checked. Front wheel toe-in should also be checked, this operation being described in **Chapter 9**. The correct setting angles are given in **Technical Data** in the Appendix.

The checking and setting of front suspension castor and camber angles should be carried out at a tyre and wheel specialist service station, having special optical measuring equipment. Whenever steering geometry is checked and adjusted, and whenever the suspension mounting points shown at **A, B, C** and **D** in **FIG 7:4** are finally tightened, the car should rest on its wheels on level ground with the tyres correctly inflated. **FIG 7:6** shows the position of the castor adjusting shims between the anti-roll bar stop and the control arm.

7:7 Modification

On the Rally and Coupé versions a modified front suspension layout was adopted in which the lower suspension arms are formed by a transverse rod and a longitudinal reaction bar replacing the anti-roll bar. This new suspension is shown in **FIG 7:7**.

7:8 Fault diagnosis

(a) Wheel wobble

1 Worn hub bearings
2 Broken or weak front spring
3 Uneven tyre wear

4 Worn suspension linkage
5 Loose wheel fixings
6 Incorrect tracking

(b) Bottoming of suspension

1 Check 2 in (a)
2 Dampers not working
3 Car overloaded

(c) Heavy steering

1 Defective wheel swivels
2 Wrong suspension geometry

(d) Excessive tyre wear

1 Check 4 and 6 in (a) and 2 in (c)

(e) Rattles

1 Check 2 in (a) and 1 in (c)
2 Worn bushes
3 Damper attachments loose

(f) Excessive rolling

1 Check 2 in (a) and 2 in (b)

CHAPTER 8

REAR SUSPENSION

8:1 Description

The independent rear wheel suspension employs a transverse leaf spring controlled by telescopic hydraulic dampers. On saloon cars, a two-leaf spring is used, a three-leaf unit being specified for estate car models. The spring is mounted on silentbloc rubbers to prevent road vibration from being transmitted to the car body. Wheel vertical movement is controlled by pressed steel control arm assemblies which pivot on fixings mounted on the car body, these fixings having provision for adjustment in order to set the rear wheel geometry. **FIG 8:1** shows the layout of the rear suspension system.

8:2 Rear hubs

The rear wheel hubs are supplied complete with bearings and the complete assembly must be renewed if bearings are defective.

Raise the rear of the vehicle and support safely on stands. Remove the wheels. Remove the hub cap with tool A.47014. Unscrew the wheel centring stud and the drum attachment screw and remove the brake drum. Unscrew the hub nut and remove the washer. Use tool A.47017 to remove the hub complete with bearing.

Reassemble in the reverse order to dismantling. The hub nut must be tightened to 101 lb ft and the nut collar crimped as described in **Section 7:3**.

8:3 Rear spring

Removal:

Refer to **FIG 8:2**. Raise the rear of the car and support it safely on floor stands. Remove the two silentblocs on the outer fixing points of the transverse spring main leaf. Disconnect the brake limiter control unit. Remove the fixing brackets on the guide stirrups. Remove the transverse spring assembly from the car.

Inspect the springs for cracks or breakage and that contact surfaces are smooth. Check the interleaf shim and rubber pads for wear. Renew as necessary.

Refitting:

Refitting is a reversal of the removal procedure.

8:4 Rear dampers

Removal:

Raise and safely support the rear of the car. Remove the road wheel. Remove the fixing screw from the top of the damper unit which is located inside the luggage compartment. Disconnect the handbrake cable from beneath the car, then detach the damper lower fixings and remove the damper from the car.

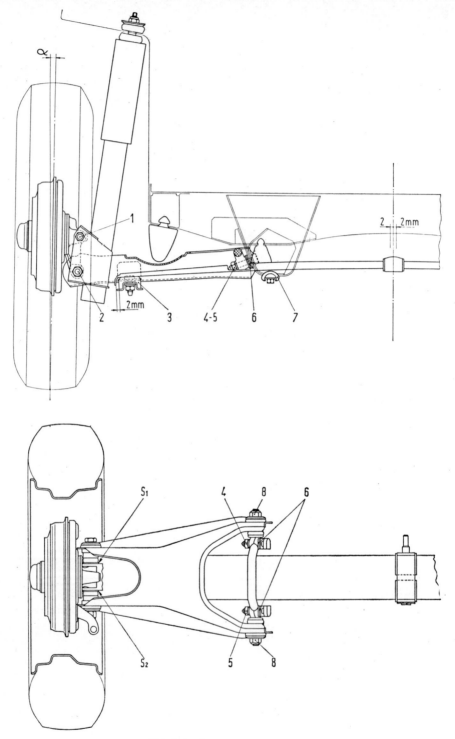

FIG 8:1   Rear suspension layout

Key to Fig 8:1   1 Knuckle to damper nut   2 Damper and control arm to knuckle nut   3 Rubber buffer   4 and 5 Control arm to body screws and nuts   6 Shims   7 Leaf spring guide   8 Control arm pivot bar nuts   **S1** and **S2** Shims

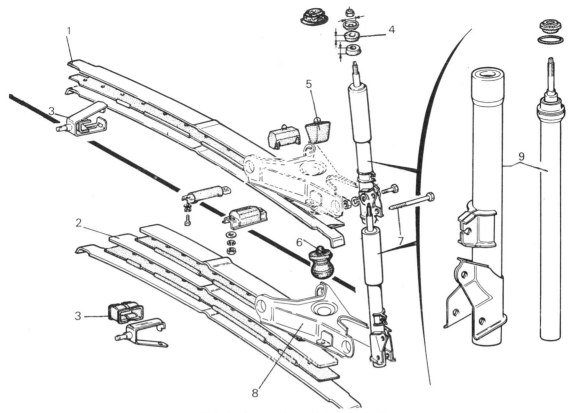

FIG 8:2   Rear spring and damper details

Key to Fig 8:2   1 Leaf spring assembly, saloon cars   2 Leaf spring assembly, estate cars   3 Guide stirrups   4 Damper upper attachment   5 and 6 Rubber buffers   7 Lower strut bolt   8 Control arm   9 Suspension strut assembly and damper unit

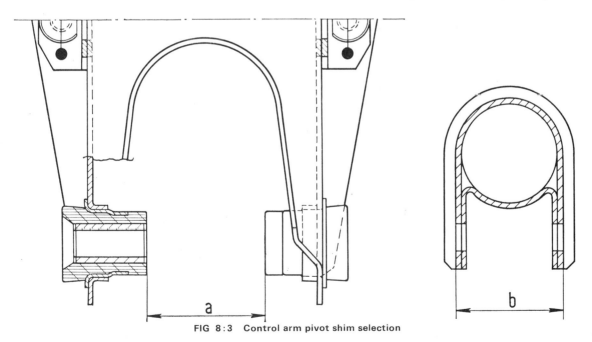

FIG 8:3   Control arm pivot shim selection

Refitting:

This is a reversal of the removal procedure. When tightening the lower damper retaining nut to the specified torque of 58 lb ft, note that the car must be standing on its wheels as described in **Section 8:5**. This nut is shown at 2 in **FIG 8:1**.

8:5 Rear wheel geometry

Every 10,000 kilometres as part of normal servicing, whenever suspension components have been dismantled, or at any time when uneven tyre wear has been noted, the rear suspension toe-in and camber angles should be checked. The correct setting angles are given in **Technical Data** in the Appendix.

The checking and setting of the angles should be carried out at a tyre and wheel specialist service station using special optical measuring equipment. Whenever the geometry is checked and adjusted, and whenever the lower damper attaching nuts are finally tightened after servicing, the car should rest on its wheels on level ground with the tyres correctly inflated. Also, the centre line of the leaf spring must coincide with the centre line of the body, within 2 mm, and a clearance of 2 mm is to be left between the rubber buffers 3 and the end bending of the lower spring leaf. Adjustment of the suspension angles is carried out by adding or removing shims at points 6 and at **S**1 and **S**2, as shown in **FIG 8:1**.

To determine the thickness of shims **S**1 and **S**2 required, carry out the following instructions, referring to **FIG 8:3**.

Measure the distance 'a' between the control arm bushings, then measure the width 'b' of the damper mounting. The difference 'a' minus 'b' plus .118 inch (3 mm) will give **S**1+**S**2. **S**1 equals **S**2 plus or minus .020 inch (.5 mm). A proper tool must be used to insert shims.

8:6 Fault diagnosis

(a) Wheel wobble

1 Worn hub bearings
2 Worn control arm bushings
3 Uneven tyre wear
4 Loose wheel fixings
5 Incorrect wheel geometry

(b) Bottoming of suspension

1 Broken or weak leaf spring
2 Ineffective dampers
3 Rebound rubbers worn or missing
4 Car overloaded

(c) Rattles

1 Worn bushings
2 Damper attachments loose

(d) Excessive tyre wear

1 Check 2 and 5 in (a)

CHAPTER 9

THE STEERING GEAR

9:1 Description

Rack and pinion steering is employed on all models. The pinion shaft is turned by the lower end of the steering column shaft and moves the rack to the left or right, transmitting the steering motion to the front wheels by means of the tie-rods and the steering arms on the wheel swivels. The rack and pinion are held in mesh by a spring and plate, the spring pressure being adjustable by means of shims. The rack moves in Vulcolan bushes. The steering gear housing is held to front bodywork by clamps fitted with rubber bushes. The steering column shaft is in two parts, fitted with cardan universal joints. The tie-rod ends are connected to the wheel swivels by means of ball joint assemblies, threaded sleeves being provided to allow for front wheel toe-in adjustment.

9:2 Maintenance and lubrication

Ball joints:

The steering gear and suspension ball joints should be inspected every 5000 kilometres or whenever inspection of the underbody is carried out. Examine the ball joint rubber caps for splits, holes or other damage and renew them if not in perfect condition. The new caps must be filled with Fiat W 90/M oil prior to installation. At the same time, check the ball joints for excessive play. If evidence of looseness is found, the ball joint in question must be renewed, no servicing being possible as they are sealed assemblies. Apart from the inspections described, no maintenance or lubrication of the ball joints is required.

Steering gear:

No routine maintenance is required on the rack and pinion assembly, apart from checking the condition of the rubber gaiters which seal the assembly and making sure that their retaining clips are tight. If a rubber gaiter is split or perished, it must be renewed at once. The clips which retain the rubber gaiters must be fitted as shown in **FIG 9:1,** with the clamp screw correctly positioned. Tighten the clamp securely to ensure an oiltight joint. Later modified rubber gaiters are not fitted with clips at the outer ends which have been altered to ensure a perfect seal.

If the steering gear has been dismantled, or if a damaged gaiter or loose clip has resulted in a loss of lubricant, .140 litre of Fiat W90/M or SAE.90 oil should be injected through the rubber sleeve on the steering side, by means of a suitable syringe. **Never use grease to lubricate the steering gear.**

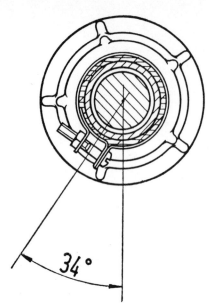

34°

9:3 Steering wheel removal

Set the steering gear to the straight-ahead position. Disconnect the battery. Remove the horn bar by removing the two screws which retain it to the steering wheel spokes, these being located on the back of the wheel. Disconnect and detach the horn contact mechanism. Remove the central steering wheel retaining nut, then pull off the steering wheel, using a suitable puller tool if necessary. Note the position of the steering wheel on the shaft for correct refitting.

Refitting:

This is a reversal of the removal procedure, making sure that the steering wheel is correctly located on the shaft. Tighten the steering wheel retaining nut to 36 lb ft torque.

9:4 Steering column

Removal:

Disconnect the battery. Remove the steering wheel as described previously. Remove the plastic covers from the upper steering column and disconnect the lighting, ignition switch and direction indicator units (see FIG 9:2. Mark the position of the lower steering column clamp relative to the pinion shaft, then remove the clamp screw. Remove the nuts and washers securing the steering column bracket to the body dash panel and the toe-board plate, then remove the steering column assembly, pulling the column shaft from the pinion shaft splines.

Servicing:

Dismantle the steering column assembly into the order shown in FIG 9:2. Thoroughly clean all parts and examine them for wear or damage, renewing any faulty components. Check the splines for burrs or distortion.

Check the universal joint assemblies for slackness, testing in both directions. The joints may be dismantled and new bearing assemblies installed if excessive wear is detected. When servicing is completed, reassemble the steering column units in the reverse order of dismantling.

Refitting:

This is a reversal of the removal procedure, aligning the marks made during removal to ensure that the steering gear is properly centralized in the straight-ahead position.

9:5 Rack and pinion assembly

Removal:

Remove the self-locking nuts from the steering gear ball joints and detach the ball joints from the arms on the wheel swivels. Remove the clamp bolt and nut from the lower steering column to pinion shaft clamp. Remove the attaching bolts which hold the steering gear clamps to the body panel, then remove the clamps and rubber grommets. Carefully remove the rack and pinion assembly, complete with tie rods and ball joints.

Dismantling:

FIG 9:2 shows the steering gear components, FIG 9:3 a section through the rack and pinion units. Loosen the locknuts and remove the tie rod ends, counting the number of turns taken to unscrew them so that they can be refitted in their original positions. This will simplify front wheel tracking, on completion. Loosen the clamps and remove the rubber gaiters. Unscrew the rack adjuster plate screws evenly, then remove them and withdraw the adjuster, spring and shim. Remove the pinion coverplate and withdraw the pinion shaft and upper bearing, collecting the gasket, seal and shim. Remove the tie rods and pressure springs from the rack, then slide the rack out of the housing.

Servicing:

Thoroughly clean all parts and examine them for wear or damage. Check the rubber gaiters for splits, holes or perished conditions and check that their fixing clamps are in good order. Check the bearings for wear by pressing and turning them by hand. Check the Vulkolan bushes in the housing for wear or scored surfaces and that the rack moves smoothly in the bushes without excessive play. If necessary, the bushes can be expelled from the ends of the housing and new bushes inserted, they being locked in position by means of a pointed screw. Check the rack for wear or damage, chipped teeth and damaged threads. Check that the crimping on each ball joint locknut does not show any sign of free play. If these nuts are removed, they must be discarded and new nuts fitted when reassembling. Under no circumstances must the old nuts be re-used. Check the rack yoke for wear or scoring and the pinion for chipped teeth or other damage.

When fitted to the rack, the tie rods must move freely in all directions on their ball joints. The adjusters must be tightened so that the tie rods will not drop under their own weight when the assembly is held horizontally.

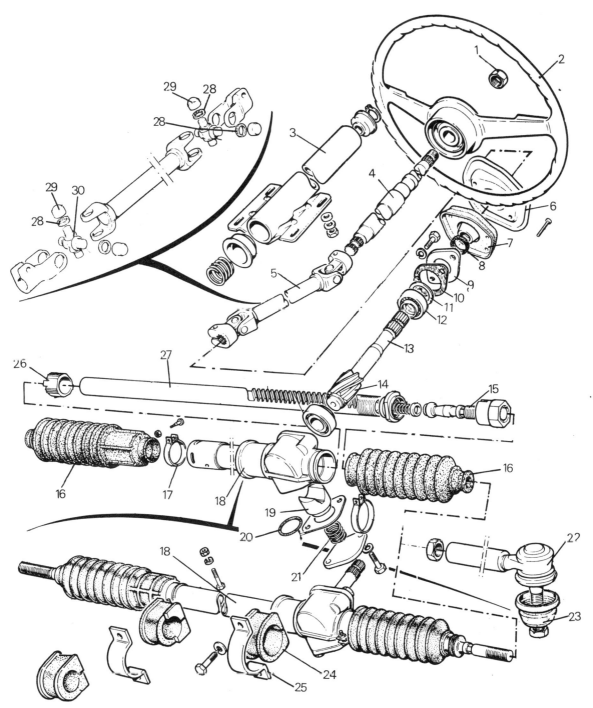

FIG 9:2   Steering gear components

Key to Fig 9:2   1 Steering wheel nut   2 Steering wheel   3 Steering column housing   4 Steering inner column, upper
5 Steering inner column, lower   6 Toe-board plate   7 Seal plate   8 Seal   9 Coverplate   10 Gasket   11 Shim
12 Upper pinion bearing   13 Pinion shaft   14 Pinion   15 Tie rod   16 Rubber gaiter   17 Gaiter clamp   18 Steering gear
housing   19 Rack yoke and adjuster   20 Shim   21 Spring   22 Tie rod end   23 Ball joint   24 Mounting bush
25 Mounting clamp   26 Rack bush   27 Rack   28 Seal   29 Bearing cap   30 Universal joint spider

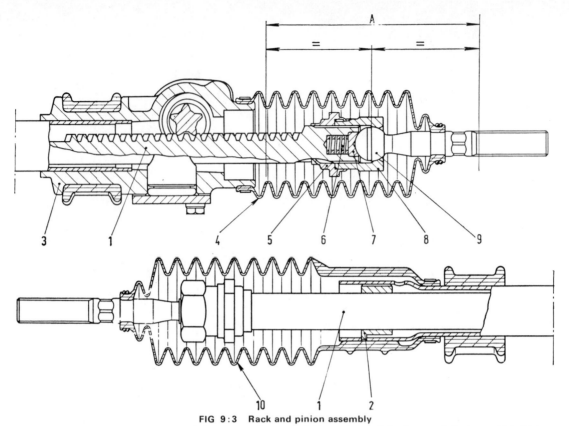

FIG 9:3   Rack and pinion assembly

Key to Fig 9:3   1 Rack   2 Bush   3 Steering housing   4 Rubber gaiter   5 Locknut   6 Spring   7 Ball joint seat
8 Tie rod   9 Ball joint adjuster   10 Rubber gaiter   **A** Shows the rack travel of 5.118 inch (130 mm)

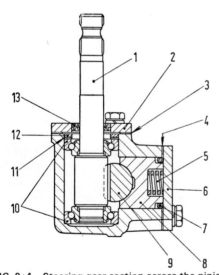

FIG 9:4   Steering gear section across the pinion

Key to Fig 9:4   1 Drive pinion shaft   2 Pinion bearing
coverplate   3 Gasket   4 Rack yoke shims   5 Spring
6 Rack yoke coverplate   7 Seal ring   8 Rack yoke   9 Rack
10 Drive pinion bearings   11 Bearing shims   12 Spacer
13 Pinion shaft seal

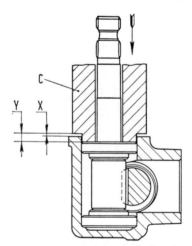

FIG 9:5   Adjusting the pinion bearings

All parts found worn or damaged during inspection must be renewed. Always use new gaskets and seals during reassembly, and observe complete cleanliness to avoid the entry of dirt or grit into the assembly.

Reassembly and adjustments:

Suitably support the steering gear housing in a horizontal position with the cover face upwards. Fit the pinion lower bearing in the housing lower bore. Engage the smooth end of the rack into the supporting sealing bush, turning the rack as necessary to facilitate this operation. Turn the rack to bring the teeth toward the centre line of the pinion seat. Fit the pinion and upper bearing, engaging it with the rack teeth. **FIG 9:4** shows a section through the assembly. The pinion must now be adjusted by selecting appropriate shim thickness in the following manner.

Refer to **FIG 9:5**. Using the special gauge **C,** apply a load of 20 lbs (9 kg) on the outer race of the upper bearing as shown. Use feeler gauges to measure the dimension **X**. A suitable shim **S** must be selected so that $S = Y - (X) + .025$ to .013 mm. Apply some sealing paste to the cover, shims and the cover fixing screws, then assemble the components and check the movement of the rack, which must show no signs of sticking during its entire travel. Move the rack to the straight-ahead steering position, centred on the length of the housing, then fit the rack yoke and adjuster spring. The rack yoke must then be adjusted in the following manner.

Refer to **FIG 9:6**. Apply a pressure of 110 lbs (50 kg) on the adjuster spring as shown and use feeler gauges to measure the gap at **Z**. A suitable shim **S** must be selected so that $S = Z + .05$ to .13 mm. Starting from the central position, turn the pinion 180 deg. in each direction during the measuring procedure. Fit the yoke shim and cover components and again check the rack for free movement. The torque required to start turning the pinion should be between 1.5 and 2 lb ft.

Fit the tie rods to the rack and set the ball joint adjusters as described in the servicing instructions given previously. Fit the pinion sealing joint, taking care not to damage the joint when sliding it over the splines. It is advised that the splines be wrapped with adhesive tape to avoid damage. Refit the rubber gaiters and the tie rod ends, if removed, screwing the tie rod ends onto the tie rods the number of turns counted during removal.

Refitting:

Check that the steering gear mounting bushes are in good condition, renewing them if they are perished or damaged. Fit the steering gear assembly into position on the car, complete with the tie rods and rubber gaiters. Fill the gear with lubricant as described in **Section 9:2**. Turn the pinion shaft until it reaches its stop, anti-clockwise on lefthand drive models, clockwise on right-hand drive models. Move the steering wheel spoke to a position within the zone **D** in **FIG 9:7** on lefthand drive models. The spoke position for righthand drive vehicles will be at a 'mirror image' position (lower right) of that shown. With the pinion and steering wheel in the positions stated, connect the steering column shaft to the pinion shaft and lock the joint with the clamp bolt and nut. On completion, check and adjust the front wheel toe-in setting as described in the next section.

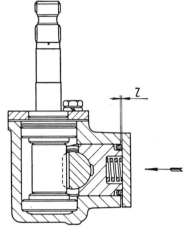

FIG 9:6   Adjusting the rack yoke

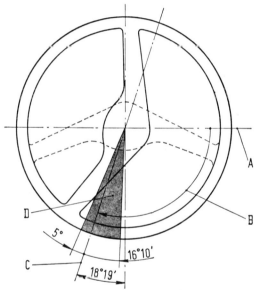

FIG 9:7   Steering wheel position for steering gear attachment. Lefthand drive models shown

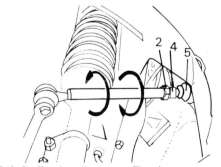

FIG 9:8   Toe-in adjustment. The sleeves on each side must be turned equally until the setting is correct

9 : 6 Wheel alignment

The correct settings are given in **Technical Data**. Whilst it is preferable to use the correct equipment for this operation, a satisfactory result may be obtained by the following method.

Inflate the tyres to the recommended pressures, and with the car on level ground, set the steering to the straightahead position. Carefully measure the distance between the inner wheel rims, at the front and at wheel-centre height. Mark the two positions with chalk. Roll the car forward for one-half a wheel revolution so the marks are at the rear of the wheels. Measure again the distance between the marks. For correct alignment the second measurement (at the rear of the wheels) should be greater or smaller than the first measurement (at the front of the wheels) according to whether toe-in or toe-out is required.

If adjustment is required, proceed as follows:

Refer to **FIG 9 : 8** and loosen the locknuts 2 on the tie rods. Rotate the two threaded sleeves 4 equally as shown until the specified alignment is obtained. Lock the nuts and recheck.

9 : 7 Fault diagnosis

(a) Wheel wobble

1 Unbalanced wheels and tyres
2 Slack steering connections
3 Incorrect steering geometry
4 Excessive play in steering gear
5 Faulty suspension
6 Worn hub bearings

(b) Heavy steering

1 Check 3 in (a)
2 Very low tyre pressures
3 Neglected lubrication
4 Wheels out of track
5 Rack adjustment too tight
6 Inner steering column shaft bent
7 Steering column bearing tight

(c) Wander

1 Check 2, 3 and 4 in (a)
2 Uneven tyre pressures
3 Uneven tyre wear
4 Ineffective dampers

(d) Lost motion

1 Loose steering wheel, worn splines
2 Worn rack and pinion teeth
3 Worn ball joints
4 Worn swivel hub joints
5 Worn universal joints
6 Slack pinion bearings

CHAPTER 10

THE BRAKING SYSTEM

10:1 Description

The braking system follows conventional practice, with hydraulically-operated disc brakes on the front wheels, self-adjusting drum brakes on the rear wheels and a cable-operated handbrake linkage which operates on the rear brakes only. A brake pressure regulating valve, operated mechanically through a rod and bar connected to the rear suspension leaf spring, reduces the pressure to the rear brakes according to the pitch of the car to minimise the possibility of the rear wheels locking under heavy braking.

The general layout of the braking system is shown in **FIG 10:1**. The master cylinder, which draws fluid from the reservoir 7, is operated from the brake pedal by a short pushrod and coupling. Separate outlets from the master cylinder are coupled, via the brake pipes, to the disc brake caliper at each front wheel. A third outlet feeds the pipelines to the rear brake units, via the pressure regulating valve. The front and rear brake circuits are operated simultaneously, but independently, from the two separate fluid chambers of the master cylinder. This dual circuit system is provided as a safety factor as, if one circuit should fail for any reason, the remaining circuit will provide effective braking power.

10:2 Routine maintenance

Regularly check the level of the fluid in the master cylinder reservoir shown in **FIG 10:2** and replenish if necessary. Wipe dirt from around the cap before removing it and check that the vent hole in the cap is unobstructed. If frequent topping up is required the system should be checked for leaks, but it should be noted that, with disc brake systems, the fluid level will drop gradually over a period of time, due to the movement of caliper pistons compensating for friction pad wear. The recommended brake fluid is Fiat blue label. **Never use anything but the recommended fluid.**

Checking brake pads and linings:

New disc brake friction pads have a thickness of 12.5 mm, the total thickness of pad and backplate being 17.5 mm. Check the friction pads on both front wheels at 5000 kilometre intervals. Raise and support the front of the car and remove both road wheels. Examine the friction pads and, if any pad has worn to a thickness of 7 mm (including backplate) or if any pad is cracked or oily, all four friction pads must be renewed. **Do not renew pads singly or on one side of the car only as uneven braking will result.**

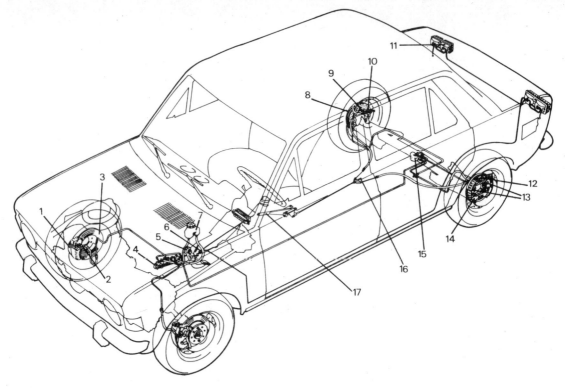

FIG 10:1   Layout of the braking system

Key to Fig 10:1   1 Front disc brake caliper   2 Front brake line bleeder connection   3 Front brake disc   4 Master cylinder
5 Service brake pedal   6 Stoplights switch   7 Brake fluid reservoir   8 Rear brake drum   9 Rear brake line bleeder connection
10 Rear brake shoes operating lever (controlled by hand lever 17)   11 Stoplights   12 Rear wheel cylinder   13 Shoe-to-drum
clearance automatic take-up device   14 Drum brake shoes   15 Brake action compensator on rear circuit   16 Handbrake
cable tensioner   17 Handbrake lever

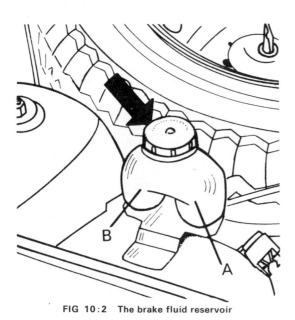

FIG 10:2   The brake fluid reservoir

New drum brake shoe linings have a thickness of 4.5 mm. Check the linings on both rear wheels at 10,000 kilometre intervals. Raise and support the rear of the car and remove both rear road wheels, then check the thickness of the linings through the two openings provided in the brake drums. If any lining has worn to a thickness of 1.5 mm, or if any lining is damaged or oily, all four rear brake linings should be renewed.

Brake adjustment:

No adjustments are required for the service brakes. The front disc brakes are self-adjusting, due to the action of the operating pistons in the calipers. These pistons are returned to the rest position after each brake operation by the piston seals, the seals being slightly stretched during brake application. As the friction pads wear, the piston stroke is increased and the piston will .travel further than before and move through the stretched seal a little, the seal returning the piston to a new position nearer the pads when the brakes are released. In this manner the piston stroke remains constant regardless of the thickness of the friction pads.

Rear drum brakes are provided with self-adjusting mechanisms which move the brake shoes nearer to the brake drums according to the amount of wear on the friction linings. This adjustment will normally maintain the handbrake adjustment correctly, but if the handbrake cable has stretched in service, or if the mechanism has been reassembled after overhaul, the handbrake should be adjusted in the following manner.

Chock the front wheels and raise the rear of the car so that the wheels are clear of the ground. Fully release the handbrake. Slacken the locknut on the brake adjuster beneath the car, as shown in **FIG 10 : 3**. Pull the handbrake lever up five clicks on the rachet and turn the adjusting nut until the rear wheels begin to bind when turned by hand. Release the handbrake and pull the lever up by three clicks. Adjust the nut further, if necessary, so that the rear wheels cannot be turned by hand. Lubricate the cable at the point where it passes through the adjuster channel so that it can move freely and allow equal pressure to be passed to the brake units. Release the handbrake fully and check that the rear wheels are free to turn without binding, then retighten the locknut and lower the car.

Earlier models with cable and outer sleeve are adjusted in a similar manner.

10 : 3 Disc brakes

FIG 10 : 4 shows a section through a typical front disc brake caliper, **FIG 10 : 5** the disc brake assembly and front hub components. The removal and maintenance of the hub assemblies is described in **Chapter 7, Section 7 : 3.** The disc brakes on the front wheels are of the non-compensating type and comprise a single hollow piston 4 within the caliper cylinder 5, sealed against fluid pressure by the rubber seal 3 and against the ingress of dirt by the rubber boot 2. Forward motion of the piston is transmitted to one brake pad 6, while reaction to this pressure on one side of the brake disc pulls the opposite pad 7 onto the other side of the disc. In this manner, equal pressure is applied by each pad on the disc surface.

Disc brake pad renewal:

Set the handbrake, raise the front of the car and safely support it on floor stands. Remove the road wheel. Remove the locking block retaining clips (see **FIG 10 : 6**) and the top and bottom locking blocks (see **FIG 10 : 7**). Remove the caliper from its mounting without disconnecting the flexible brake hose. Remove the brake pads from the caliper as shown in **FIG 10 : 8**. Mark the pads for correct refitting if they are not to be renewed.

Check the disc for run-out by mounting a dial indicator in a suitable position to register 2 mm from the outer circumference of the disc. The maximum run-out should be no more than .15 mm. If run-out exceeds this figure the disc will have to be removed and refaced, but the resulting thickness must not be less than 9.35 mm. The minimum permissible thickness through wear is 9 mm.

Check the condition of the pad springs in their housings. **FIGS 10 : 9** and **10 : 10** show the pad springs. Push the piston down in the caliper to the bottom of its bore, noting that this will cause the fluid level in the reservoir to rise and that it may be necessary to siphon off a little of the fluid to prevent spillage. Place the pads in their housings, engage the caliper locking spring and refit the caliper in its bracket as shown in **FIG 10 : 11**. Slide the blocks between the caliper body and the bracket

FIG 10 : 3   The handbrake cable adjuster

and lock them in position with the retainers. Pump the brake pedal several times to adjust the brake before using for the first time, to ensure that the piston is moved close to the pads. If this is not done the brakes may not work the first time that they are used. Check the fluid level in the supply reservoir and top up if necessary.

Servicing a caliper:

Remove the brake pads and dismount the caliper as just described. Disconnect the flexible hose from the caliper and plug the end of the hose to prevent fluid loss (see **FIGS 10 : 4** and **10 : 5**). Clean the outside of the caliper assembly with hot water and FIAT LDC detergent, rinse clean with hot water alone and dry with an air jet. Dismantle the caliper assembly into the order shown in the illustration and clean all internal parts with the correct grade of brake fluid. Do not use any other cleaning fluid or solvent. Examine for signs of wear or scoring on the cylinder and piston surfaces. Renew all

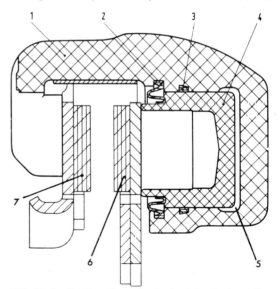

FIG 10 : 4   Section through a typical disc brake caliper

Key to Fig 10 : 4   1 Caliper body   2 Piston protection cap   3 Seal   4 Piston   5 Cylinder   6 Moving friction pad   7 Fixed friction pad

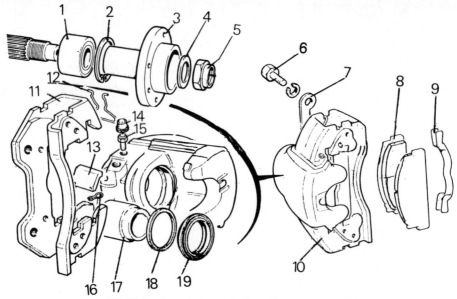

FIG 10:5   Front hub and brake caliper components

Key to Fig 10:5   1 Bearing   2 Circlip   3 Front hub   4 Lockwasher   5 Nut   6 Caliper bolt   7 Caliper bracket
8 Brake pads   9 Pad spring   10 Caliper assembly   11 Caliper bracket   12 Spring   13 Caliper locking block   14 Dust cap
15 Bleed screw   16 Retaining clip   17 Piston   18 Seal   19 Dust cover

rubber seals and dust boots and any other part found defective during inspection. Dip the internal parts in clean brake fluid and assemble them wet. Observe absolute cleanliness to prevent the entry of dirt or any trace of oil or grease. Use the fingers only to fit the rubber piston seals to prevent damage.

Refit the caliper assembly as described previously and, on completion, bleed the front brakes as described in **Section 10:7.**

10:4 Drum brakes

FIG 10:12 shows the components of the rear drum brake assembly and rear hub. The removal and maintenance of the hub assemblies is described in **Chapter 8, Section 8:2.**

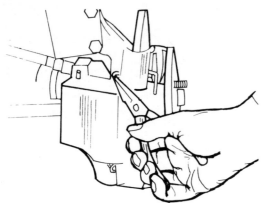

FIG 10:6   Removing the block retaining pins

Removing the brake shoes:

Chock the front wheels, jack-up the rear of the car, remove the road wheels and fully release the handbrake. Remove the brake drum to expose the brake shoe assemblies. Release the brake shoe hold-down pins 2 by depressing the cap and turning through 90 deg. Disconnect the upper and lower brake shoe return springs, noting their positions for correct refitting. Clamp the wheel cylinder to prevent inadvertent ejection of the pistons. Turn hub cut-out in turn to each adjuster 8 for clearance when removing shoes. Pull the shoe assemblies outwards to detach the ends from the anchor plate and wheel cylinder, then remove the shoes, taking care not to allow grease or oil to contaminate the friction linings.

Compress adjuster in clamp A.72246 and remove the retaining circlip. Release the clamp slowly and collect the plain and friction washers, the spring and casing. Check that a load of 92 to 110 lb is required to compress the spring to 9.5 mm.

Refitting:

This is a reversal of the removal procedure, making sure that the shoes are firmly seated into the wheel cylinder and anchor plate. On completion, operate the brakes several times so that the shoes adjust themselves to the correct working clearance.

Relining brake shoes:

It is not recommended that owners attempt to reline brake shoes themselves. It is important that the linings be properly bedded to the shoes and ground for concentricity with the brake drum. For this reason it is best to obtain sets of replacement shoes on an exchange

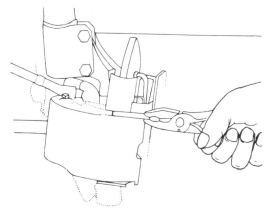

FIG 10:7 Removing the top and bottom locking blocks

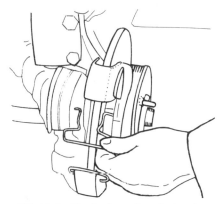

FIG 10:9 The brake pad control spring

basis, or have the shoes relined at a service station. **Do not allow grease, oil or brake fluid to contaminate brake linings. If the linings are contaminated in any way they must be renewed as they cannot be successfully cleaned.**

Servicing a wheel cylinder:

Remove the rear brake shoes as just described. Disconnect the flexible hose from the rear of the wheel cylinder and plug the end of the hose to prevent fluid loss. Remove the two retaining screws and detach the wheel cylinder from the brake backplate. The wheel cylinder components are shown in **FIG 10:14.** Dismantle the cylinder assembly into the order shown, discard the rubber boots and seals and thoroughly clean all remaining parts in the correct grade of brake fluid. Inspect the pistons and cylinder bores for signs of scoring or rust marks which would dictate renewal. If the pistons do not slide freely in the cylinder, carefully polish the sliding surfaces.

Reassembly is a reversal of the dismantling procedure, using new rubber parts. Coat all parts with clean brake fluid and assemble them wet, using the fingers only to fit rubber seals and caps to prevent damage. Refit the cylinder to the brake backplate and install the shoes and drum as described previously. On completion, bleed the rear brakes as described in **Section 10:7.**

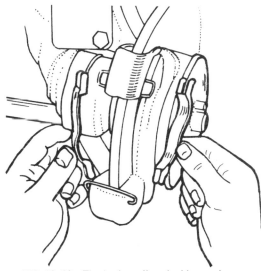

FIG 10:10 The brake caliper locking springs

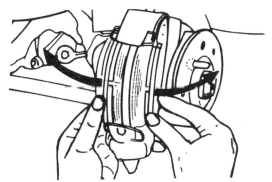

FIG 10:8 Removing the brake pads

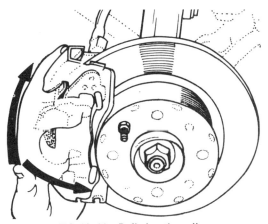

FIG 10:11 Refitting the caliper

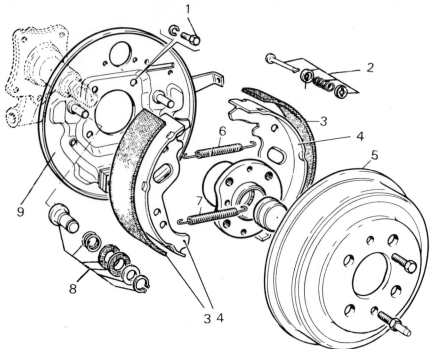

FIG 10:12   Rear hub and drum brake components

Key to Fig 10:12   1 Backplate screw   2 Shoe hold down pin assembly   3 Brake lining   4 Brake shoe   5 Brake drum
6 Upper shoe return spring   7 Lower shoe return spring   8 Brake adjuster assembly   9 Backplate

10:5 The master cylinder

Removal:

Remove the reservoir cap and plug the outlets to the master cylinder.

Disconnect the supply reservoir feed pipes and the brake supply pipes from the master cylinder. Remove the two master cylinder retaining screws, then move the master cylinder forward to clear the pedal pushrod and lift the unit from the car.

Servicing:

Refer to **FIG 10:14**. Remove the boot from the end of the cylinder, screw out the stop screws as necessary and remove the end plug, slide out all parts noting their

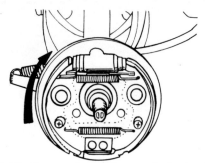

FIG 10:13   The rear brake shoes and wheel cylinder. The arrow shows the direction of forward wheel rotation

positions for reassembly. Discard all rubber parts and thoroughly clean the remaining parts in the correct grade of brake fluid. Inspect all parts for scoring, wear or damage. Make sure that the compensating ports in the body are clear. Check the pistons and cylinder bores for rust marks or scoring, which would dictate renewal of the affected component. Always renew any part if its serviceability is in doubt.

Coat all parts with clean brake fluid and assemble them wet. Preassemble the secondary piston assembly and insert it into the master cylinder bore, retaining by tightening the stop screw. Refit the primary piston and all other components in the reverse order of dismantling. Use only the fingers to fit the new rubber parts to prevent damage.

Refitting:

This is a reversal of the removal procedure. On completion, top up the fluid in the supply reservoir to the correct level, then bleed all the brakes as described in **Section 10:7**

10:6 Brake regulator

The rear wheel brake regulator comprises a piston, operated from a linkage connected to the rear leaf spring, which operates in a cylinder. The movement of the piston is controlled by the state of rear spring deflection and varies the flow of brake fluid to the rear wheel cylinders when the brakes are applied, to prevent rear wheel locking under heavy braking conditions. **FIG 10:15** shows

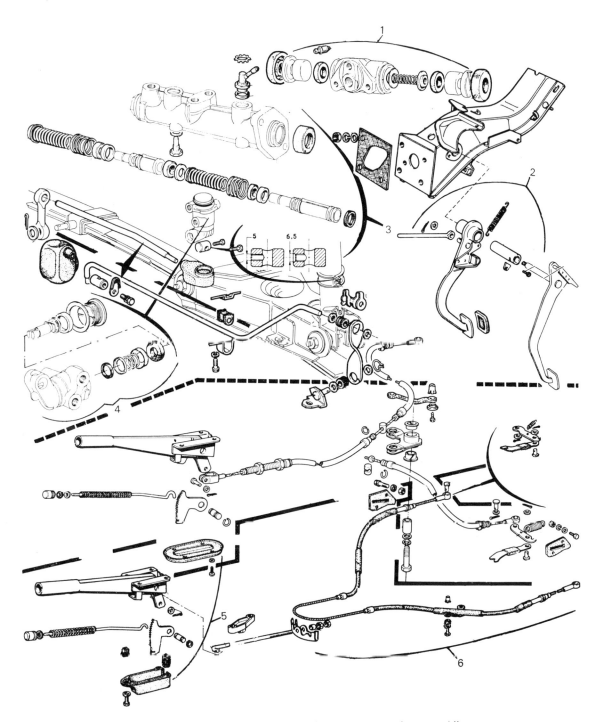

FIG 10:14 Components of the braking system operating assemblies

Key to Fig 10:14   1 Wheel cylinder assembly   2 Brake pedal assembly   3 Master cylinder assembly   4 Brake regulator assembly   5 Handbrake lever assembly   6 Handbrake cable and connections

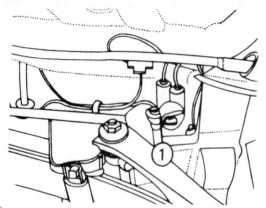

FIG 10:15 Location of the brake regulator unit

the location of the brake regulator assembly beneath the car, **FIG 10:16** sections through the regulator while at rest and while under heavy braking conditions.

Application of the brakes causes the rear of the car body to rise by an amount consistent with the degree of retardation, this movement causing a change in the amount of rear leaf spring compression. This rear spring movement is transmitted to the regulator by the connecting torsion bar 1. The short crank which has been bearing on the end of the regulator piston then moves away from it and the piston moves under the pressure of fluid from the master cylinder.

Up until this moment, the piston has been positioned by the torsion bar crank so that there is a free flow around its head, and the seal 6 is clear of the transfer ports in the slotted ring 7. Under these conditions, any brake pressure supplied is transmitted equally to all four brake units. When the piston moves outwards as described, it first closes the main transfer route around its head and under the seal, then, by taking the seal with it, closes the more restricted transfer ports in the slotted ring. Any further increase in pressure from the master cylinder cannot be applied to the rear brakes, all effort being concentrated on the front brake units. The rear brakes are still, however, held partially applied as the fluid previously trapped in the brake pipes cannot return.

As braking effort is reduced, the rear leaf springs return to a normal position and the torsion bar exerts pressure on the piston to re-open, first, the main transfer route around the head and under the seal, and then, by moving the seal clear of the transfer ports in the slotted ring, the secondary route. After this gradual return to the normal position, brake pressure is then once more equalized on all four wheels.

Adjustment:

Early type (see FIG 10:17):

Remove splitpin and washer and disconnect link T from linkpin H, leave the link hanging. Measure the distance X from the bottom of the linkpin hole to the top of the linkpin. The measurement should be 30 to 32 mm with the car unloaded and a full fuel tank.

The regulator bracket is slotted at nut B to allow for adjustment. Reconnect link to linkpin.

Later type (see FIG 10:18):

Disconnect torsion bar 3 from link 4. Set end of torsion bar 3b 54 ± 5 mm from centre of rubber buffer mounting hole 2. Lift boot 9 and check that the end of the torsion bar at 3a is in light contact with the piston 8. If necessary loosen screws 7 and reposition regulator. Tighten screws 7 to 18 lb ft torque. Reconnect link and torsion bar.

10:7 Bleeding the system

This is not routine maintenance and is only necessary if air has entered the system due to parts being dismantled, or because the fluid level in the supply reservoir has been allowed to drop too low. The need for bleeding is indicated by a spongy feeling of the brake pedal accompanied by poor braking performance. This must not be confused with the sharp drop in brake efficiency accompanied by greater pedal travel which indicates that one of the dual braking circuits has failed. This latter condition must be investigated immediately and the fault rectified.

If work has been carried out on the front brakes only or the rear brakes only, then it will normally only be necessary to bleed the circuit (front or rear) that is affected,

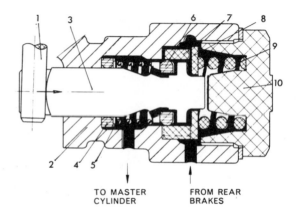

TO MASTER CYLINDER   FROM REAR BRAKES

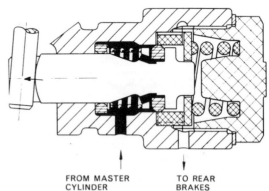

FROM MASTER CYLINDER   TO REAR BRAKES

FIG 10:16 Section through the brake regulator while at rest, above, when braking hard, below

Key to Fig 10:16   1 Cranked end of torsion bar
2 Regulator body   3 Piston   4 Piston seal   5 Sealing washer and spring   6 Sealing ring   7 Slotted ring
8 Ring retaining washer   9 Washer retaining spring
10 End plug and washer

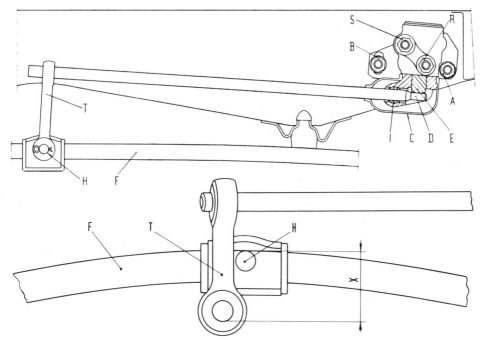

FIG 10:17 Early type regulator adjustment

Key to Fig 10:17   A, B Regulator attaching nuts   C Dust boot   D Piston end of torsion bar   E Regulator piston   F Leaf spring   H Link anchor pin to leaf spring   I Regulator pin   R, S Brake fluid line connectors   T Torsion bar link to leaf spring

as the other system should not have been disturbed. If both circuits have been disturbed, or if braking performance is poor, bleeding must be carried out at all four wheels. Bleeding must be carried out in the following sequence: left rear wheel, right rear wheel, right front caliper, left front caliper. **Do not bleed the brakes with any drum or caliper removed, or with any brake line disconnected.** The only exception to this rule is when bleeding front brakes with the calipers removed as described at the end of this section.

Do not bleed the rear wheel systems while the rear suspension is unloaded as this would cause the regulator to operate and make bleeding the system difficult. If the wheels are removed to facilitate the bleeding operation, place a jack under the spring to load it.

Check the fluid level in the supply reservoir and top up if necessary. Clean the bleed screw dust caps and the area around the bleed screws to remove all dirt and rust. Remove the cap from the appropriate bleed screw and attach a length of rubber tube to the screw as shown in **FIG 10:19**. Lead the free end of the tube into a transparent container and add sufficient brake fluid to safely cover the end of the tube. Loosen the bleed screw and have an assistant press the brake pedal quickly to the floor and allow it to return slowly. Repeat the operation until no air bubbles can be seen in the fluid flowing from the tube into the container. Check the fluid level in the supply reservoir frequently during the procedure to ensure that the level does not drop too low. When the fluid is free from air bubbles, hold the pedal to the floor at the end of a down stroke and tighten the bleed screw. Refit the dust cap and proceed to the next wheel.

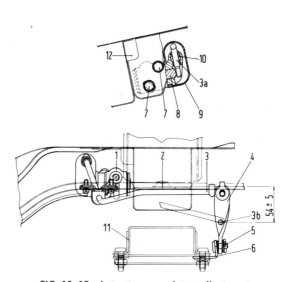

FIG 10:18 Later type regulator adjustment

Key to Fig 10:18   1 Brake pressure regulator   2 Buffer housing   3 Torsion bar   3a Regulator end of torsion bar   3b Anchor rod end of torsion bar   4 Torsion bar link to control arm   5 Link anchor pin to control arm   6 Link anchor pin bracket   7 Brake pressure regulator attaching and adjusting screws   8 Regulator piston   9 Dust boot   10 Regulator pin   11 Control arm   12 Brake pressure regulator mounting bracket

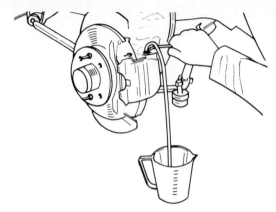

FIG 10:19   Bleeding the brakes

If, after bleeding the brakes as stated, the pedal still feels spongy, repeat the operation on the front brakes, removing each caliper in turn and lifting it so that the bleed screw is higher than the flexible hose elbow. This procedure will release any air trapped inside the caliper. Refit each caliper before bleeding the other. When bleeding calipers in this manner, it is essential that a metal or hardwood plate, the thickness of the brake disc, be fitted between the brake pads in the caliper. If this is not done, the pads will move too close together and allow the piston to release from its bore. On completion, refit the caliper as stated in **Section 10:3,** pushing the piston to the bottom of its bore by pulling the pads apart.

Discard all dirty fluid. As a general rule, it is best to discard all fluid bled from the system if its condition is at all doubtful. Always store brake fluid in clean, sealed containers.

10:8 Master Vac servo unit

On some models before 1976, and on all later cars a vacuum servo unit of the Master Vac type is incorporated in the braking system. This is bolted on to the engine bulkhead and operated directly by the brake pedal in the case of lefthand drive cars. On righthand drive cars a relay rod running across the car transmits the movement from the brake pedal to the Master Vac which continues to be mounted on the left. The master cylinder is bolted to the front face of the servo unit.

The inclusion of the servo unit in no way affects the layout or operation of the brake system, it simply permits greater pressure to be applied at the master cylinder than that exerted by the driver on the brake pedal. This is achieved by utilizing the vacuum in the inlet manifold to act on a diaphragm/piston assembly in a sealed cylinder in a degree proportional to the movement of the brake pedal. This piston then acts directly on the master cylinder pushrod and so operates the wheel brake units with augmented pressure.

The design of the Master Vac is so arranged that, in the event of a failure in the vacuum supply, a mechanical connection is retained between the brake pedal and the master cylinder so that full braking efficiency is still available but higher pedal pressure is required.

No maintenance should be required on the servo unit and no adjustment is required in normal service. If it is removed at any time, or if the master cylinder is removed, the gap between the operating rod and the master cylinder thrust plate must be set to the following dimensions:

Rally models   .05 to .07 in (1.26 to 1.85 mm)
128S and SL models   .04 to .05 in (1.05 to 1.26 mm)

10:9 Fault diagnosis

(a) Spongy pedal

1 Leak in the system
2 Worn master cylinder
3 Leaking wheel or caliper cylinders
4 Air in the fluid system
5 Gaps between brake shoes and underside of linings

(b) Excessive pedal movement

1 Check 1 and 4 in (a)
2 Excessive lining or pad wear
3 Very low fluid level in supply reservoir

(c) Brakes grab or pull to one side

1 Distorted discs or drums
2 Wet or oily pads or linings
3 Loose backplate or caliper
4 Disc or hub loose
5 Worn suspension or steering connections
6 Mixed linings of different grades
7 Uneven tyre pressures
8 Broken shoe return springs
9 Seized handbrake cable
10 Seized wheel cylinder or caliper piston

(d) Brakes partly or fully locked on

1 Swollen pads or linings
2 Damaged brake pipes preventing fluid return
3 Master cylinder compensating hole blocked
4 Master cylinder piston seized
5 Brake or pedal return spring broken
6 Dirt in the hydraulic system
7 Damaged or faulty regulator mechanism
8 Seized wheel cylinder or caliper piston
9 Seized drum brake adjusters

(e) Brake failure

1 Empty fluid reservoir
2 Broken hydraulic pipeline
3 Ruptured master cylinder seal
4 Ruptured wheel cylinder or caliper seal

(f) Reservoir empties too quickly

1 Leaks in pipelines
2 Deteriorated cylinder seals

(g) Pedal yields under continuous pressure

1 Faulty master cylinder seals
2 Faulty wheel cylinder or caliper seals

CHAPTER 11

THE ELECTRICAL SYSTEM

11:1 Description

All models covered by this manual have 12-volt electrical systems in which the negative terminal of the battery is earthed to the car bodywork.

There are wiring diagrams in Technical Data at the end of this manual which will enable those with electrical experience to trace and correct faults.

Instructions for servicing the items of electrical equipment are given in this chapter, but it must be pointed out that it is not sensible to try to repair units which are seriously defective, electrically or mechanically. Such faulty equipment should be replaced by new or re-conditioned units which can be obtained on an exchange basis. Some models are fitted with generator charging systems, others with alternator systems.

11:2 The battery

To maintain the performance of the battery it is essential to carry out the following operations, particularly in winter when heavy current demands must be met.

Keep the top and surrounding parts of the battery dry and clean, as dampness can cause current leakage. Clean off corrosion from the metal parts of the battery mounting with diluted ammonia and coat them with anti-sulphuric paint. Clean the terminal posts and smear them with petroleum jelly, tightening the terminal clamps securely. High electrical resistance due to corrosion at the battery terminals can be responsible for a lack of sufficient current to operate the starter motor.

Every month or 2500 kilometres, whichever occurs first, remove both covers from the battery, as shown in FIG 11:1 and check the electrolyte level in each cell, topping up with distilled water if necessary, to just cover the separators.

If a battery fault is suspected, test the condition of the cells with a hydrometer. **Never add neat acid to the battery. If it is necessary to prepare new electrolyte due to loss or spillage, add sulphuric acid to distilled water. It is highly dangerous to add water to acid. It is safest to have the battery refilled with electrolyte, if it is necessary, by a service station.**

The indications from the hydrometer readings of the specific gravity are as follows:

For climates below 27°C or 80°F:	*Specific gravity*
Cell fully charged	1.270 to 1.290
Cell half discharged	1.190 to 1.210
Cell discharged	1.110 to 1.130

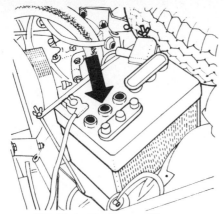

FIG 11:1   The battery filler caps

FIG 11:2   Circuit diagram for the generator

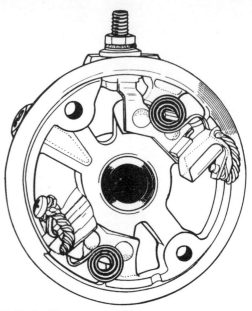

FIG 11:3   The generator end plate, showing the brushes held in the raised position

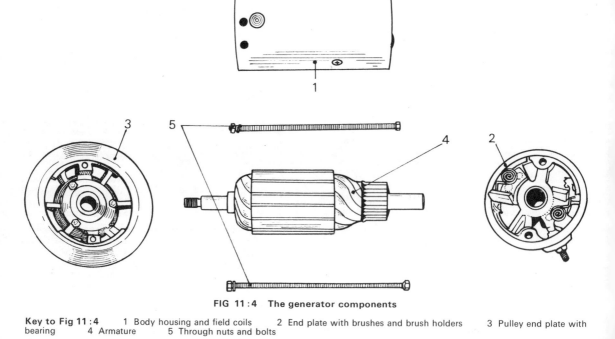

FIG 11:4   The generator components

Key to Fig 11:4   1 Body housing and field coils   2 End plate with brushes and brush holders   3 Pulley end plate with bearing   4 Armature   5 Through nuts and bolts

For climates above 27C° or 80°F:

Cell fully charged	..	..	.. 1.210 to 1.230
Cell half discharged	..	..	.. 1.130 to 1.150
Cell discharged	..	..	.. 1.050 to 1.070

These figures assume an electrolyte temperature of 60°F or 16°C. If the temperature of the electrolyte exceeds this, add .002 to the readings for each 5°F or 3°C rise. Subtract .002 for any corresponding drop below 60°F or 16°C.

All cells should read approximately the same. If one differs radically from the others it may be due to an internal fault or to spillage or leakage of the electrolyte.

If the battery is in a low state of charge, take the car for a long daylight run or put the battery on a charger at 5 amps, with the filler caps removed, until it gases freely. Do not use a naked light near the battery as the gas is inflammable. If the battery is to stand unused for long periods, give a refreshing charge every month. It will be ruined if it is left uncharged.

11:3 The generator

The generator is a shunt wound two-pole unit, type D.90.12.16.3E and is used with an independent voltage regulator.

The armature is mounted in single-row ballbearings at each end, which require no lubrication in normal service. If dismantled at any time the bearings must be packed with FIAT MR3 grease. The carbon brushes are mounted in reaction brush holders.

The generator is mounted on a clamp support on the side of the engine and the pulley shares a common vee-belt drive with the water pump. Adjustment of this belt is covered in **Chapter 4, Section 4:4**.

Two terminals are provided, one mounted on the end cap at the brush end, marked 51 and providing the positive output to the system and the other, mounted on the generator body and marked 67, provides the negative connection to the shunt field winding. The negative connection is through the earthed generator case, as shown in **FIG 11:2**.

Little in the way of routine maintenance is needed on the generator. A check on belt tightness is all that is required. After a number of years in service, the generator may need attention in regard to two points, brush renewal and commutator skimming. Both operations are quite straightforward and can be carried out with the minimum of tools.

With the generator removed from the car and the generator drive pulley extracted, wipe the exterior clean and transfer the unit to the bench. Remove the two nuts securing the through-bolts at the rear end of the unit and withdraw the bolts. The end plates will then be retained entirely by the flange edges in the main body.

Working through the apertures in the commutator end plate, lift the springs clear of the brushes, raise the brushes and let the springs fall back onto the sides of the brushes to hold them in the raised position in the brush holders, as shown in **FIG 11:3**. Now remove the end plate from the body, sliding the armature shaft out of the bearing.

Gently tapping the end of the armature shaft vertically on the bench, push out the opposite end plate from the body with the armature still held in the ballbearing.

FIG 11:5 Checking commutator runout with a dial gauge

Extract the armature from the end plate leaving the ball-bearing in place. Loosen and remove the nuts securing the ballbearing retainer plate and remove the plate. Extract the bearing from its seating. The dismantled generator components are shown in **FIG 11:4**.

Inspect all parts for wear or damage. In particular, examine the surfaces of the armature and the faces of the polepieces in the body for evidence of rubbing. Extract the carbon brushes from their holders and disconnect the flexible leads from the terminal plates. Examine the commutator for signs of wear or scoring and if necessary clean it up in accordance with the instructions given below.

Examine the armature windings and field coil windings for signs of overheating. If this is present, or if one of the commutator segments shows evidence of arcing at the edge (usually a sign of an open circuit in one winding) it is best to obtain a replacement unit from a service station.

Thoroughly clean all parts and, if necessary, fit new carbon brushes to the end plate. If the commutator shows excessive wear, mount it in a lathe and skim, taking fine cuts with a sharp tool while the armature is rotated at not less than the service speed of 9000 rev/min. Remove only sufficient metal to clean up. Finish off with fine sandpaper and check for roundness on vee-blocks as shown in **FIG 11:5**. The out of round must not exceed .0004 inch. This is important because at the high speeds attained by the armature under service conditions, any eccentricity, however small, will cause the brushes to oscillate and bounce, burning both brushes and commutator and seriously reducing their life.

Finally, undercut the mica insulation between the commutator segments to a depth of 1 mm, using a special saw or a hacksaw blade ground to the correct thickness, then polish the segments and wipe away all dust.

Reassemble the unit, packing the ballbearing with MR3 grease and, as the last operation, lower the brushes onto the commutator and reposition the springs to hold them down.

Use only the specified Fiat brushes for the generator. These are made to a precise specification. Any change in brush quality will affect the performance of the generator

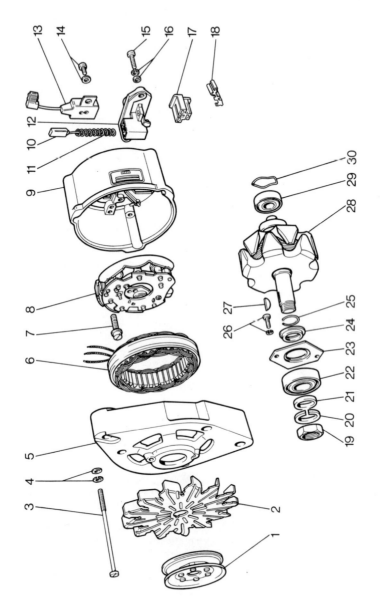

FIG 11:6 Components of the alternator

Key to Fig 11:6 1 Pulley 2 Fan 3 Through-bolt 4 Spring and plain washers 5 Drive end cover 6 Stator 7 Screw
8 Diode carrier 9 Casing 10 Brush 11 Spring 12 Brush holder 13 Field diode 14 Screw and washer 15 Screw
16 Spring and plain washers 17 Terminal block 18 Connector 19 Nut 20 Spring washer 21 Thrust ring 22 Bearing
23 Bearing retainer plate 24 Thrust ring 25 Circlip 26 Screw and spring washer 27 Woodruff key 28 Rotor 29 Bearing
30 Spring clip

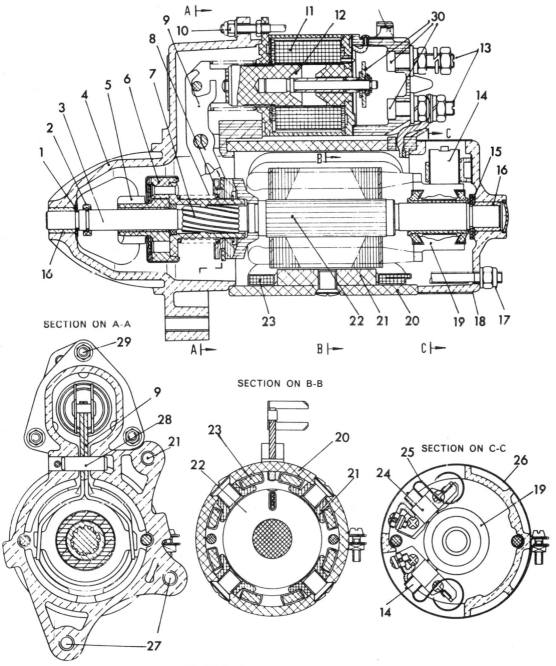

FIG 11:7   Starter motor components

Key to Fig 11:7   1 Washers   2 Snap ring   3 Armature shaft   4 Mounting end plate   5 Engagement drive pinion   6 Clutch   7 Splines   8 Sleeve   9 Operating lever   10 Solenoid attachment nuts   11 Solenoid winding   12 Solenoid armature   13 Heavy current terminals   14 Brush   15 Washers   16 Bush   17 Through-bolt and nut   18 Commutator end plate   19 Commutator   20 Body housing   21 Polepiece   22 Armature winding and laminations   23 Field coil   24 Brush holder   25 Brush spring   26 Commutator end cover   27 Holes for fixing to bellhousing   28 Pivot pin   29 Solenoid attachment bolts   30 Heavy duty switch contacts

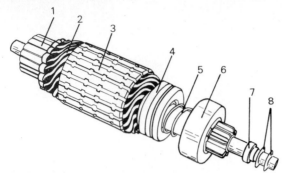

FIG 11:8   Starter motor armature and drive

Key to Fig 11:8   1 Commutator   2 Windings
3 Laminations   4 Sleeve   5 Spring   6 Clutch and spur
7 Snap ring   8 Washers

and regulator assemblies which are particularly sus-
ceptible to small changes in circuit resistance. The faces
of new brushes are already set to the curvature of the
commutator, therefore bedding-down operations should
not be necessary.

11:4   The alternator

The alternator which is fitted to later models is shown
in **FIG 11:6**. The advantage of an alternator over a direct
current generator is that it has greatly improved low
speed output and a higher maximum operating speed
and total output. The current produced by the unit is
alternate, this being rectified to a direct current supply
by diodes mounted in the alternator case. Alternator drive
is taken from the vee-belt which drives the engine water
pump. Apart from an occasional check on drive belt
tension as described in **Chapter 4, Section 4:4**, very
little maintenance is required. Every 60,000 miles, or
more frequently in dusty conditions, the alternator rotor
slip rings on which the brushes operate should be cleaned
carefully with a dry cloth and the complete brush holder
assembly renewed.

The alternator must never be run with the battery disconnected, nor must the battery cables be reversed at
any time. Test connections must be carefully made, and
the battery and alternator wiring must be completely
disconnected before any electric welding is carried out
on any part of the car. These warnings must be observed,
otherwise extensive damage to the alternator components, particularly the diodes, will result.

Due to the complexity of equipment required to
adequately test and service the alternator it is recommended that, if the performance is suspect, the car be
taken to a service station for specialist attention.

11:5   The starter

The Fiat E.84-0.8/12 starter, fitted to all models, is a
brush-type series wound motor equipped with an over-
running clutch and operated by a solenoid. The armature
shaft is supported in sintered metal bushes which are
factory-packed with lubricant and require no servicing
between overhauls. **FIG 11:7** shows the starter motor
components.

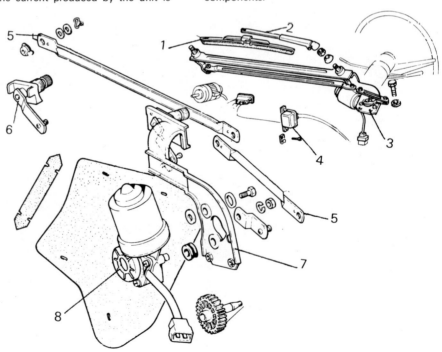

FIG 11:9   The windscreen wiper motor and linkage

Key to Fig 11:9   1 Wiper blade   2 Wiper arm   3 Wiper linkage   4 Relay   5 Connecting rods   6 Wiper heads
7 Mounting plate   8 Wiper motor

When the starter is operated from the switch, the engagement lever moves the pinion into mesh with the engine flywheel ring gear. When the pinion meshes with the ring gear teeth, the solenoid contact closes the circuit and the starter motor operates to turn the engine. When the engine starts, the speed of the flywheel causes the pinion to overrun the clutch and armature. The pinion continues in engagement until the engagement lever is released, when it returns to the rest position under spring action.

Tests for a starter which does not operate:

Check that the battery is in good condition and fully charged and that its connections are clean and tight. Switch on the headlamps and operate the starter switch. Current is reaching the starter if the lights dim when the starter is operated, in which case it will be necessary to remove the starter for servicing. If the lights do not dim significantly, switch them off and operate the starter switch while listening for a clicking sound at the starter motor, which will indicate that the solenoid is operating.

If no sound can be heard at the starter when the switch is operated, check the wiring and connections between the battery and the starter switch and between the switch and the solenoid. If the solenoid can be heard operating when the starter switch is operated, check the wiring and connections between the battery and the main starter motor terminals, taking care not to accidentally earth the battery to starter motor lead. If the wiring is not the cause of the trouble, the fault is internal and the starter motor must be removed and serviced.

Removing the starter:

Disconnect the battery and remove the front bottom trays from beneath the car. Disconnect the starter leads from their terminals. Remove the three fixing screws which hold the starter to the engine block, then withdraw the unit, sliding it horizontally to the left.

Refitting is a reversal of this procedure.

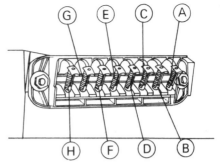

FIG 11:10 A later type fusebox. The circuits covered are described in the text

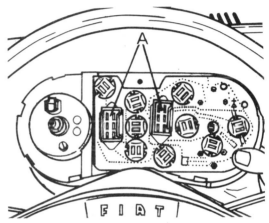

FIG 11:11 Instrument cluster removal. The two electric connectors are shown at A

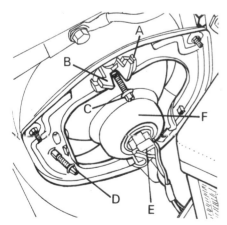
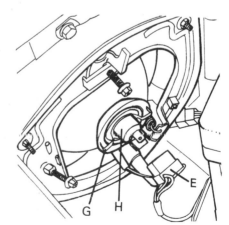

FIG 11:12 Headlamp mounting details

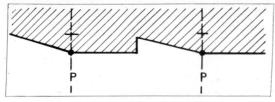

FIG 11:13 Headlamp aiming diagram

Key to Fig 11:13   +=height of lamp centre above ground
P=specified distance (see text) below cross for centre of beam

Dismantling the starter:

Disconnect the lead from the solenoid winding by unscrewing the fixing nut. Unscrew the three nuts securing the solenoid in position, then remove the solenoid.

Remove the cover from the commutator end of the motor and disconnect the positive brush from the winding lead. Lift both brushes and use their springs to retain them, in the manner described earlier for generator brushes. Remove the nuts from the through-bolts at the commutator end and slide the end plate clear of the body. Take care not to lose the thrust washers.

Remove the split pin and pivot pin from the drive engagement lever, then ease the armature, complete with the forked engagement lever, out of the casing together with the thrust washers. Remove the fork from the engagement sleeve. The armature assembly is shown in **FIG 11:8.** If it is necessary to dismantle the drive components, remove the washers 8, extract the snap ring 7 and slide off the remaining parts.

Reassembly:

After inspecting all parts and renewing any found worn or damaged, reassemble the starter in the reverse order of dismantling. When reassembling the drive, lubricate the splines with Fiat VS.10W oil or equivalent, and the spindle bushes with engine oil. If it is necessary to skim the commutator, refer to the procedure described earlier for generator armatures, the methods being the same.

11:6 Windscreen wiper

The windscreen wiper is controlled by a switch on the dashboard and is an electro-mechanical unit which operates the wiper arms through a linkage system.

If wiper operation is sluggish, check the linkage for binding. If the motor is inoperative, check the fuse first, then check the wiring and connections between the battery and switch and between the switch and wiper motor. If the motor unit is defective, an exchange unit should be obtained and fitted. **FIG 11:9** shows the components of the wiper and linkage assemblies.

Removing a wiper blade:

Tilt out the wiper arm, free the blade from its locking dowel on the arm, then remove the blade upwards. Refit in the reverse order.

Removing the wiper mechanism:

Remove the wiper blades. Remove the screws and sealing caps from the wiper heads, then remove the plate assembly fixing screws and remove the plate assembly. Refitting is a reversal of the removal procedure.

11:7 Fuses

These are located in a box, fitted with a snap-on cover, underneath the instrument panel. Early cars had nine 8 amp fuses and one 16 amp, later cars have seven 8 amp and one 16 amp fuses, see **FIG 11:10.** The circuits protected are as follows:

Fuse No. (early cars):

1 Horns, Cooling fan, Interior lights (16 amps).
2 Windscreen wiper, Heater fan.
3 Lefthand high beam and high beam warning.
4 Righthand high beam.
5 Lefthand low beam.
6 Righthand low beam.
7 Lefthand side, Righthand tail, boot and number plate lamps.
8 Righthand side, Lefthand tail and engine compartment lamps.
9 Stop and flasher lights, Gauges.
10 Spare.

Fuse No. (later cars):

1(A) Flashers and stop, Windscreen wiper, Gauges.
2(B) Horns, Cooling fan, Interior lights (16 amps).
3(C) Lefthand high beam and high beam indicator.
4(D) Righthand high beam.
5(E) Lefthand low beam.
6(F) Righthand low beam.
7(G) Lefthand side, Righthand tail and number plate. Instrument lights.
8(H) Righthand side, Lefthand tail and number plate. Engine compartment.
9   16 amp optional. Heated rear window.

Always check the fuse concerned first, whenever electrical faults are encountered in the circuits listed. If the fuse has blown, check the wiring and connections for possible shortcircuits and items of electrical equipment for internal shorts and correct the fault before fitting a new fuse of the correct type. If a fuse has blown due to an accidental shortcircuit caused when working on the electrical system, or if a temporary overload has occurred, no electrical tests need be made before fitting the new fuse. To avoid accidental shortcircuits, it is wise to disconnect the battery before working on any part of the electrical system, however small. It is also advisable to carry spare fuses of each type in the car, as a blown fuse on a journey can be most inconvenient, particularly at night. A useful tip to remember, if a fuse has blown and no new replacement is available is to transfer a good fuse

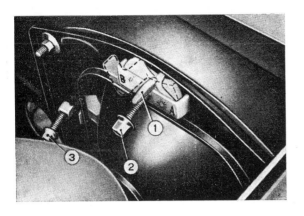

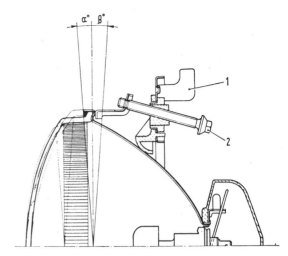

FIG 11:14   System for adjusting headlamp beam elevation to compensate for vehicle loading

Key to Fig 11:14   1 Height adjustment lever   2 Vertical adjustment screw   3 Horizontal adjustment screw   Position A: for empty or part-laden car   Position B: for fully loaded car   Angle $\alpha = \beta = 4$ deg.

from one of the circuits not in use at the time to the circuit which has failed. For example, if the fuse protecting the wiper circuit should fail during daylight driving, the fuse protecting circuits **G** could be substituted temporarily after the fault in the first circuit **A** has been corrected.

11:8 Instrument cluster

The instrument cluster is retained to the dash panel by a single screw at its lower edge. To remove the cluster, take out this screw, pull the cluster forward for access, then disconnect the speedometer cable and the two connectors shown at **A** in **FIG 11:11.** Bulbs can then be removed as required, pushing and turning to disconnect them from the bayonet fixings.

11:9 Headlamps

Several different headlamp installations are used in the various cars covered by this manual. The standard equipment is a pair of conventional circular tungsten units of the type shown in **FIG 11:12.**

On Rally models four Halogen units are used of which the inner units provide the main beam and the outer units the dipped beam.

The 128S has two rectangular units providing main and dipped beams by the use of double filament lamps, while 128SL models have four circular tungsten units in which all four are used for main beam and the two outboard units only for dip.

Replacing a bulb:

The bulb H is reached, on the standard fitting, from inside the engine compartment. To change a defective bulb, pull off the socket E, rubber boot F and release the spring retainer G by rotating the holder anticlockwise at the same time pushing in slightly. Pull out the bulb.

Fit the spring retainer on to the new bulb ensuring that the location dowel for correct aiming is in register with its socket. Fit the rubber boot F so that its slot is aligned

with the parking light. Finally fit the socket connector on to the lamp terminals.

Setting the headlamp beam:

This is preferably carried out at a service station with the correct optical equipment. If this is not possible, an acceptable degree of accuracy can be obtained by using the following method.

Refer to **FIG 11:13.** Place the car, unladen, on level ground and facing a wall or board at a distance of 5 metres (16 feet). Mark on the wall two (four on 128SL and Rally models) crosses + at lamp centre height from the ground and the correct distance apart. The reference point P represents the centre of the high intensity area of the headlamp beam when switched on and the distance of P below the cross varies according to vehicle type. These dimension are as follows:

128 standard models	9 cm
128S models	9 cm
128SL models	9 cm (outer) 6 cm (inner)
128 Rally models	7.5 cm (outer) 2 cm (inner)

To adjust the setting of the beams rotate the adjusting screws as necessary to line them up with the aiming points. These screws are shown in the illustration as C for vertical movement and D for horizontal adjustment.

Headlamp height adjustment:

On later models in this range the device shown in **FIG 11:14** is fitted by which the height of the headlamp beam can be adjusted to compensate for the effect of varying vehicle loads

In addition to the conventional screws for normal headlamp alignment in the vertical and horizontal planes, 2 and 3, the rocking lever 1 is able to make a rapid adjustment in the vertical plane only of up to 1 degree on either side of the preset position. This is achieved by rocking the lever from position A to position B, or vice versa, for an empty or a loaded vehicle respectively.

Occasionally the seats of the screws 2 and 3 should be smeared with grease where they make contact with the headlamp. Smear also the coil springs and any other moving or rubbing parts of the adjustment system.

The angles α and β in the diagram are each equal to 4 deg. and represent the total angular movement of the lamp.

11:10 Lighting circuits

Lamps give insufficient light:

Check that the lamp units are clean. Refer to **Section 11:2** and check the condition of the battery, recharging if necessary. Check the setting of the headlamps as described in **Section 11:8** and renew any bulbs which have darkened with age.

Bulbs burn out frequently:

Have the control box settings checked by an autoelectrical service station.

Lamps light when switched on but gradually fade:

Refer to **Section 11:2** and check the battery, as it is not capable of supplying current for any length of time.

Lamp brilliance varies with the speed of the car:

Check the condition of the battery and its connections. Make sure that the connections are clean and tight and renew any faulty cables.

11:11 Fault diagnosis

(a) Battery discharged

1 Terminal connections loose or dirty
2 Shorts in lighting circuits
3 Generator or alternator not charging
4 Control box faulty
5 Battery internally defective

(b) Insufficient charge rate

1 Check 1 and 4 in (a)
2 Drive belt slipping
3 Alternator diodes defective
4 Generator defective

(c) Battery will not hold charge

1 Low electrolyte level
2 Battery plates sulphated
3 Electrolyte leakage from cracked case
4 Battery plate separators defective

(d) Battery overcharged

1 Control box faulty

(e) Generator or alternator output low or nil

1 Drive belt broken or slipping
2 Control box faulty
3 Brushes sticking, springs weak or broken
4 Faulty internal windings
5 Defective diode(s) (alternator)

(f) Starter motor lacks power or will not turn

1 Battery discharged, loose cable connections
2 Starter switch or solenoid faulty
3 Brushes worn or sticking, leads detached or shorting
4 Commutator dirty or worn
5 Starter shaft bent
6 Engine abnormally stiff, perhaps after rebore

(g) Starter runs but does not turn engine

1 Pinion engagement mechanism faulty
2 Broken teeth on pinion or flywheel gears

(h) Starter motor rough or noisy

1 Mounting bolts loose
2 Pinion engagement mechanism faulty
3 Damaged pinion or flywheel teeth

(j) Noisy starter when engine is running

1 Pinion return mechanism faulty

(k) Starter motor inoperative

1 Check 1 and 3 in (f)
2 Armature or field coils faulty

(l) Lamps inoperative or erratic

1 Battery low, bulbs burned out
2 Faulty earthing of lamps or battery
3 Lighting switch faulty, loose or broken connections

(m) Wiper motor sluggish, taking high current

1 Wiper motor internally defective
2 Lack of lubrication
3 Linkage worn or binding

CHAPTER 12

THE BODYWORK

12:1 Bodywork finish

Large scale repairs to body panels are best left to expert panel beaters. Even small dents can be tricky, as too much hammering will stretch the metal and make things worse instead of better. If panel beating is to be attempted, use a dolly on the opposite side of the panel. The head of a large hammer will suffice for small dents, but for large dents a block of metal will be necessary. Use light hammer blows to reshape the panel, pressing the dolly against the opposite side of the panel to absorb the blows. If this method is used to reduce the depth of dents, final smoothing with a suitable filler will be easier, although it may be better to avoid hammering minor dents and just use the filler.

Clean the area to be filled, making sure that it is free from paint, rust and grease, then roughen the area with emerycloth to ensure a good bond. Use a proprietary fibreglass filler paste mixed according to the manufacturers instructions and press it into the dent with a putty knife, or similar flat-bladed tool. Allow the filler to stand proud of the surrounding area to allow for rubbing down after hardening. Use a file and emerycloth or a disc sander to blend the repaired area to the surrounding

bodywork, using finer grade abrasive as the work nears completion. Apply a coat of primer surfacer and, when it is dry, rub down with 'Wet or Dry' paper lubricated with soapy water, finishing with 400 grade. Apply more primer and repeat the operation until the surface is perfectly smooth. Take time on achieving the best finish possible at this stage as it will control the final effect.

The touching up of paintwork can be carried out with self-spraying cans of paint, these being available in a wide range of colours. Use a piece of newspaper or board as a test panel to practice on first, so that the action of the spray will be familiar when it is used on the panel. Before spraying the panel, remove all traces of wax polish. Mask off large areas such as windows with newspaper and masking tape. Small areas such as trim strips or door handles can be wrapped with masking tape or carefully coated with grease or vaseline. Apply the touching up paint, spraying with short bursts and keeping the spray moving. Do not attempt to cover the area in one coat, applying several coats with a few minutes drying time between each. If too much paint is applied at one time, runs may develop. If so, do not try to remove the run by wiping, but wait until it is dry and rub down as before.

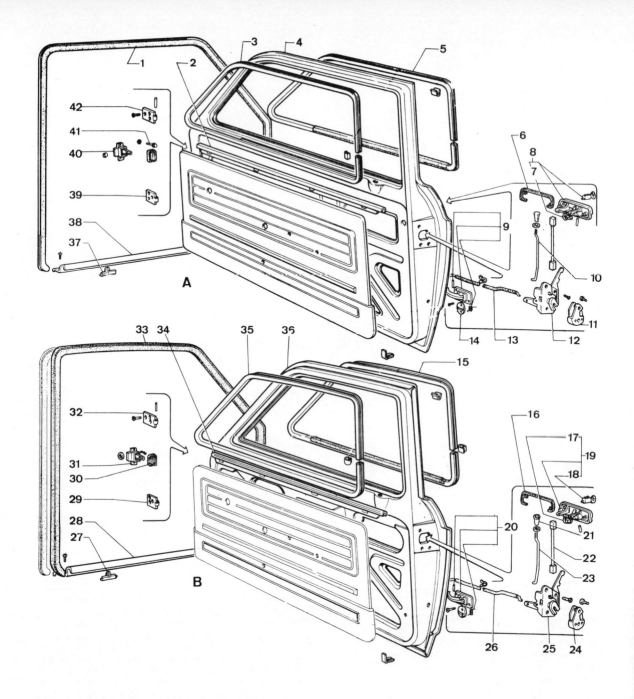

FIG 12:1 Front door components. A is the assembly used on Berline 2-door and Familiale models, B the Berline 4-door assembly

Key to Fig 12:1 1 Weatherstrip   2 Door trim retaining channel   3 Window moulding   4 Door panel   5 Window moulding   6 Lock seal   7 and 8 Door outside handle assembly   9 Door inside handle assembly   10 Lock plunger   11 Lock striker plate   12 Door lock unit   13 Operating rod   14 Escutcheon   15 Window moulding   16 Seal   17, 18 and 19 Door outside handle assembly   20 Door inside handle assembly   21 Lock plunger knob   22 Security bar   23 Lock plunger   24 Lock striker plate   25 Door lock unit   26 Operating rod   27 Clip   28 Moulding   29 Hinge   30 Grommet   31 Door check   32 Hinge   33 Weatherstrip   34 Door trim retaining channel   35 Window moulding   36 Door panel   37 Clip   38 Moulding   39 Hinge   40 Door check   41 Screw   42 Hinge

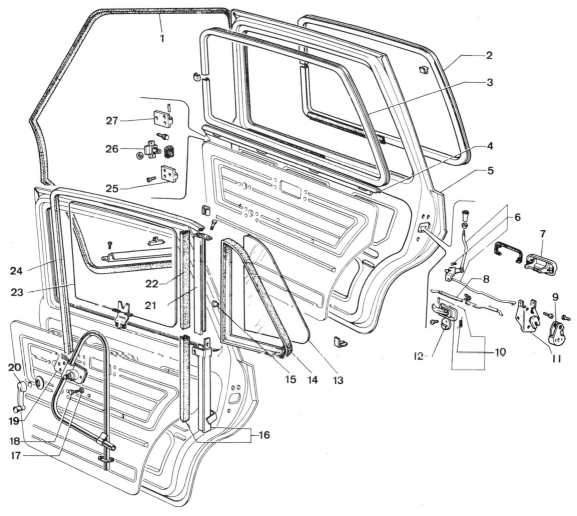

FIG 12:2   Rear door components

Key to Fig 12:2   1 Weatherstrip   2 and 3 Window moulding   4 Door trim retaining channel   5 Door panel
6 Lock plunger   7 Outside door handle   8 Operating rod   9 Lock striker plate   10 Inside door handle   11 Door lock unit
12 Escutcheon   13 Glass   14 Weatherstrip   15 Grommet   16 Glass channel   17 Washer   18 Screw
19 Regulator plate   20 Regulator handle   21 Glass channel   22 Seal strip   23 Window glass   24 Seal strip   25 Hinge
26 Door check   27 Hinge

After the final coat has been applied, allow a few hours of drying time before blending the new finish to the old with a fine cutting compound, buffing with a light, circular motion. Finish with the application of a good quality polish.

12:2 Removing door trim

Push back the trim around the window regulator handle, then use a suitable tool to pull out the escutcheon to expose the handle retaining clip. Remove the clip and detach the handle, escutcheon and spring. Take out the attaching screws and remove the armrest. Lever off the door inside release handle escutcheon and remove the ashtray, if fitted. With a screwdriver inserted between

the trim panel and the adjacent metalwork, ease the panel away from its clips and slide it clear of the door handle to remove it.

12:3 Door glass and regulator mechanism

The door windows are raised and lowered by a cable type regulator from the handle mounted on the door panel. To remove the regulator, the trim panel must first be removed from the door as described in **Section 12:2**. Wind the window fully down. **FIG 12:3** shows the attachment points for a typical window regulator mechanism. Remove the regulator mechanism fixings and detach the mounting plate from the lower glass channel, then remove the mechanism from the door

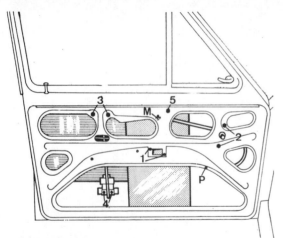

FIG 12:3 Typical window regulator mechanism attachments

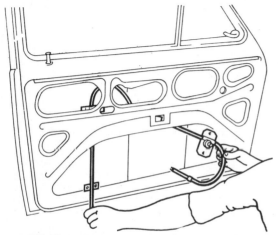

FIG 12:4 Removing the regulator mechanism

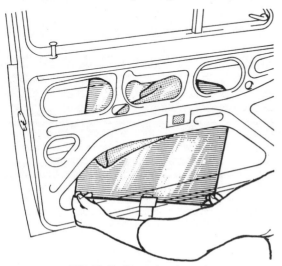

FIG 12:5 Removing door glass

panel as shown in **FIG 12:4.** The window glass must be detached from its guide channels and removed through the lower door aperture, as shown in **FIG 12:5.**

12:4 Door locks and hinges

Locks and hinges must be kept in good condition and cleaned and lightly lubricated at regular intervals. The doors are secured by locks which are operated by a handle from the outside and a lever from the inside, a safety plunger being provided at each door to secure the lock from the inside. The locks are retained to the door panel by screws, which should be checked for tightness from time to time. The lock latch plate is secured to the door jamb by screws, these screws allowing for adjustment of the plate to ensure correct door closing. The latch plates should be adjusted when necessary, to hold the door securely closed without rattle but without the need for excessive slamming to close. When properly adjusted, the joint between the door and the adjacent panel should be flush. To realign the door in the aperture if it has moved out of alignment, mark the hinge positions, loosen the hinge screws and realign the door, using the marks made as a guide when making small adjustments. Retighten the screws and check the fit of the door, resetting the latch plate if the realignment procedure has affected the proper closing of the door.

12:5 The bonnet

The bonnet over the engine compartment is hinged at the front and is fitted with a spring prop to hold it open in the vertical position, as shown in **FIG 12:6,** the rear catch being operated from a release handle and cable fitted in the car.

To remove the bonnet, scribe round the hinge plates for correct refitting, then remove the hinge mounting bolts. Have an assistant to help with the removal procedure to prevent the unit swinging onto the surrounding bodywork. Pinch the lower ends of the bonnet prop together to release it from the restraint bracket, then lift off the bonnet.

12:6 Luggage compartment and tailgate

FIG 12:7 shows the Saloon car luggage compartment lid and **FIG 12:8** the Estate car tailgate. Both units are conventionally hinged and are secured by cylinder type locks with adjustable latch plates. The luggage compartment lid is fitted with a compensating coil spring to assist the raising operation, the tailgate being fitted with a steel torsion bar for this purpose.

12:7 The facia

FIG 12:9 shows the facia components. The assembly is attached to the bodywork by screw fixings and can be removed after the instrument panel items have been disconnected. Disconnect the battery to prevent accidental shortcircuits during removal, taking out the instrument panel attaching screw, then pull the panel into the car for access to the rear. Disconnect the instruments, warning lamps and speedometer cable, then remove the instrument panel from the facia. Disconnect the wiring connections to the facia mounted switches, then unscrew and remove the facia. To remove the lower facia panel it will be necessary to disconnect the heater controls.

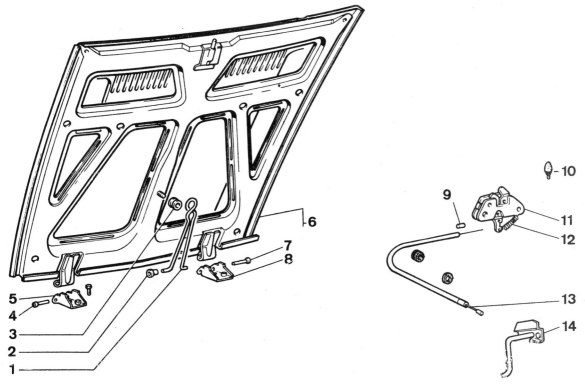

FIG 12:6 The bonnet and latch mechanism

Key to Fig 12:6   1 Bonnet prop   2 Bush   3 Bonnet prop catch   4 Pivot pin   5 Hinge plate   6 Bonnet panel
7 Pivot pin   8 Hinge plate   9 Pin   10 Rubber buffer   11 Bonnet catch   12 Spring   13 Release cable   14 Release lever

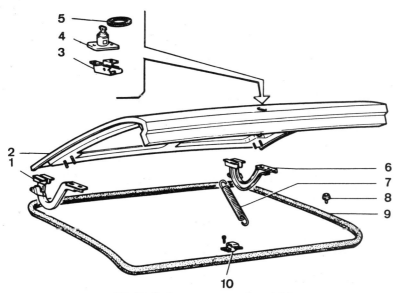

FIG 12:7 Luggage compartment lid

Key to Fig 12:7   1 Hinge   2 Luggage compartment lid   3 Coverplate   4 Lock assembly   5 Seal   6 Hinge
7 Compensating spring   8 Buffer   9 Weatherstrip   10 Striker plate

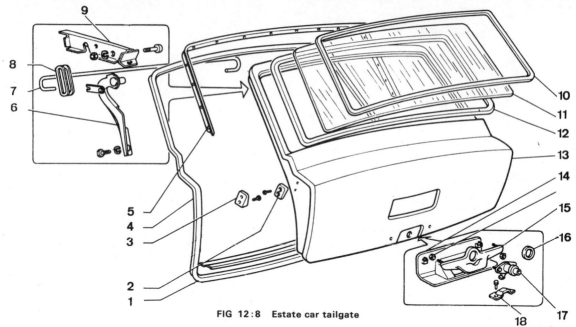

FIG 12:8 Estate car tailgate

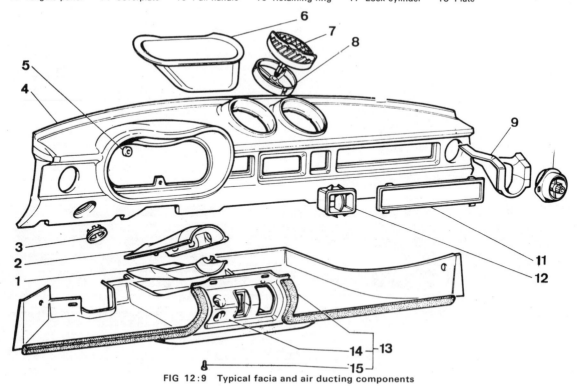

FIG 12:9 Typical facia and air ducting components

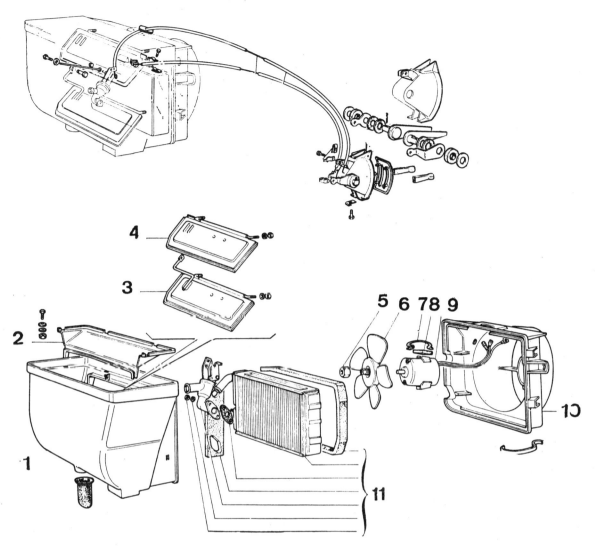

FIG 12:10   Heater and control cable assemblies

Key to Fig 12:10   1 Heater cover   2 Protector   3 and 4 Air doors   5 Nut   6 Heater fan   7 Clip   8 Seal   9 Heater motor
10 Casing   11 Heater radiator and water pipes

12:8 The heater

The heater unit is fitted at the upper rear of the engine compartment. Cable controls are provided to adjust the temperature of the incoming air, this being accomplished by mixing hot air from the heater unit with cold air from the car exterior in variable proportions, no water valve being provided. This means that the heater radiator is always at a constant temperature, ensuring immediate response to heater control changes. Air exchange within the car is provided for by the inclusion of concealed extractor slots behind the rear parcel shelf.

If heater performance is poor, check the cooling system thermostat first, as described in **Chapter 4**. If the thermostat is in good order and operates as stated, check the air doors in the heater unit and their cable operation. If this is not the cause of the trouble, the heater hoses and heater radiator unit must be checked for blockages. If the heater blower is defective, check the fuse, wiring and switch units.

The heater unit can be removed and dismantled after disconnecting the water hoses, wiring and control cables. **FIG 12:10** shows the heater components and operating mechanism.

NOTES

APPENDIX

Inches		Decimals	Milli-metres	Inches to Millimetres		Millimetres to Inches	
				Inches	mm	mm	Inches
	1/64	.015625	.3969	.001	.0254	.01	.00039
1/32		.03125	.7937	.002	.0508	.02	.00079
	3/64	.046875	1.1906	.003	.0762	.03	.00118
1/16		.0625	1.5875	.004	.1016	.04	.00157
	5/64	.078125	1.9844	.005	.1270	.05	.00197
3/32		.09375	2.3812	.006	.1524	.06	.00236
	7/64	.109375	2.7781	.007	.1778	.07	.00276
1/8		.125	3.1750	.008	.2032	.08	.00315
	9/64	.140625	3.5719	.009	.2286	.09	.00354
5/32		.15625	3.9687	.01	.254	.1	.00394
	11/64	.171875	4.3656	.02	.508	.2	.00787
3/16		.1875	4.7625	.03	.762	.3	.01181
	13/64	.203125	5·1594	.04	1.016	.4	.01575
7/32		.21875	5.5562	.05	1.270	.5	.01969
	15/64	.234375	5.9531	.06	1.524	.6	.02362
1/4		.25	6.3500	.07	1.778	.7	.02756
	17/64	.265625	6.7469	.08	2.032	.8	.03150
9/32		.28125	7.1437	.09	2.286	.9	.03543
	19/64	.296875	7.5406	.1	2.54	1	.03937
5/16		.3125	7.9375	.2	5.08	2	.07874
	21/64	.328125	8.3344	.3	7.62	3	.11811
11/32		.34375	8.7312	.4	10.16	4	.15748
	23/64	.359375	9.1281	.5	12.70	5	.19685
3/8		.375	9.5250	.6	15.24	6	.23622
	25/64	.390625	9.9219	.7	17.78	7	.27559
13/32		.40625	10.3187	.8	20.32	8	.31496
	27/64	.421875	10.7156	.9	22.86	9	.35433
7/16		.4375	11.1125	1	25.4	10	.39370
	29/64	.453125	11.5094	2	50.8	11	.43307
15/32		.46875	11.9062	3	76.2	12	.47244
	31/64	.484375	12.3031	4	101.6	13	.51181
1/2		.5	12.7000	5	127.0	14	.55118
	33/64	.515625	13.0969	6	152.4	15	.59055
17/32		.53125	13.4937	7	177.8	16	.62992
	35/64	.546875	13.8906	8	203.2	17	.66929
9/16		.5625	14.2875	9	228.6	18	.70866
	37/64	.578125	14.6844	10	254.0	19	.74803
19/32		.59375	15.0812	11	279.4	20	.78740
	39/64	.609375	15.4781	12	304.8	21	.82677
5/8		.625	15.8750	13	330.2	22	.86614
	41/64	.640625	16.2719	14	355.6	23	.90551
21/32		.65625	16.6687	15	381.0	24	.94488
	43/64	.671875	17.0656	16	406.4	25	.98425
11/16		.6875	17.4625	17	431.8	26	1.02362
	45/64	.703125	17.8594	18	457.2	27	1.06299
23/32		.71875	18.2562	19	482.6	28	1.10236
	47/64	.734375	18.6531	20	508.0	29	1.14173
3/4		.75	19.0500	21	533.4	30	1.18110
	49/64	.765625	19.4469	22	558.8	31	1.22047
25/32		.78125	19.8437	23	584.2	32	1.25984
	51/64	.796875	20.2406	24	609.6	33	1.29921
13/16		.8125	20.6375	25	635.0	34	1.33858
	53/64	.828125	21.0344	26	660.4	35	1.37795
27/32		.84375	21.4312	27	685.8	36	1.41732
	55/64	.859375	21.8281	28	711.2	37	1.4567
7/8		.875	22.2250	29	736.6	38	1.4961
	57/64	.890625	22.6219	30	762.0	39	1.5354
29/32		.90625	23.0187	31	787.4	40	1.5748
	59/64	.921875	23.4156	32	812.8	41	1.6142
15/16		.9375	23.8125	33	838.2	42	1.6535
	61/64	.953125	24.2094	34	863.6	43	1.6929
31/32		.96875	24.6062	35	889.0	44	1.7323
	63/64	.984375	25.0031	36	914.4	45	1.7717

UNITS	Pints to Litres	Gallons to Litres	Litres to Pints	Litres to Gallons	Miles to Kilometres	Kilometres to Miles	Lbs. per sq. In. to Kg. per sq. Cm.	Kg. per sq. Cm. to Lbs. per sq. In.
1	.57	4.55	1.76	.22	1.61	.62	.07	14.22
2	1.14	9.09	3.52	.44	3.22	1.24	.14	28.50
3	1.70	13.64	5.28	.66	4.83	1.86	.21	42.67
4	2.27	18.18	7.04	.88	6.44	2.49	.28	56.89
5	2.84	22.73	8.80	1.10	8.05	3.11	.35	71.12
6	3.41	27.28	10.56	1.32	9.66	3.73	.42	85.34
7	3.98	31.82	12.32	1.54	11.27	4.35	.49	99.56
8	4.55	36.37	14.08	1.76	12.88	4.97	.56	113.79
9		40.91	15.84	1.98	14.48	5.59	.63	128.00
10		45.46	17.60	2.20	16.09	6.21	.70	142.23
20				4.40	32.19	12.43	1.41	284.47
30				6.60	48.28	18.64	2.11	426.70
40				8.80	64.37	24.85		
50					80.47	31.07		
60					96.56	37.28		
70					112.65	43.50		
80					128.75	49.71		
90					144.84	55.92		
100					160.93	62.14		

UNITS	Lb ft to kgm	Kgm to lb ft	UNITS	Lb ft to kgm	Kgm to lb ft
1	.138	7.233	7	.967	50.631
2	.276	14.466	8	1.106	57.864
3	.414	21.699	9	1.244	65.097
4	.553	28.932	10	1.382	72.330
5	.691	36.165	20	2.765	144.660
6	.829	43.398	30	4.147	216.990

TECHNICAL DATA

ENGINE

Bore and stroke:
  1100 ... ...   80 mm × 55.5 mm
  1300 ... ...   86 mm × 55.5 mm

Capacity:
  1100 ... ...   1116 cc (68.10 cu inch)
  1300 ... ...   1290 cc (78.72 cu inch)

Compression ratio:
  1100 ... ...   8.8 : 1 (9.2 : 1 from 1976)
  1300 and Rally ... ...   8.9 : 1
  1300 3P ... ...   9.2 : 1

Crankshaft:

Main bearing journal diameter	1.9990 to 1.9998 inch (50.775 to 50.795 mm)
From 1977	1.9990 to 2.000 inch (50.785 to 50.805 mm)
Main bearing thickness (standard) ...	.0718 to .0721 inch (1.825 to 1.831 mm)
Main bearing running clearance	.0020 to .0037 inch (.050 to .095 mm)
From 1977	.0016 to .0033 inch (.040 to .085 mm)
Wear limit	.006 inch (.15 mm)
Main bearing undersizes	Four sizes .010 to .040 inch (.254 to 1.016 mm)
Crankshaft end float	.0021 to .0104 inch (.055 to .265 mm)
Wear limit	.014 inch (.35 mm)
Maximum journal taper	.0002 inch (.005 mm)
Crankpin diameter	1.7913 to 1.7920 inch (45.498 to 45.518 mm)

Connecting rods:

Big-end bearing thickness (standard)	.0603 to .0606 inch (1.531 to 1.538 mm)
Big-end undersizes available	Four sizes, .010 to .040 inch (.254 to 1.016 mm)
Big-end running clearance	.0014 to .0034 inch (.036 to .086 mm)
Wear limit	.004 inch (.10 mm)
Piston pin interference fit in small-end (1116 cc)	.0004 to .0017 inch (.010 to .042 mm)

Pistons:
Diameter (standard):

1100, class A	79.940 to 79.950 mm
class C	79.960 to 79.970 mm
class E	79.980 to 79.990 mm
1300, class A	85.920 to 85.930 mm
class C	85.940 to 85.950 mm
class E	85.960 to 85.970 mm
Oversizes available	+ .2, .4 and .6 mm

Piston to cylinder clearance:

1100	.0020 to .0028 inch (.050 to .070 mm)
1300	.0028 to .0036 inch (.070 to .090 mm)

Piston rings:

Ring to groove clearance (1116 cc):
- Top ring ... ... .0018 to .0030 inch (.045 to .077 mm)
- Middle ring ... ... .0010 to .0022 inch (.025 to .057 mm)
- Bottom ring ... ... .0008 to .0020 inch (.020 to .052 mm)

Ring groove clearance (1290 cc):
- Top ring ... ... .0018 to .0030 inch (.045 to .077 mm)
- Middle ring ... ... .0015 to .0028 inch (.040 to .072 mm)

Bottom ring ... ... .0012 to .0024 inch (.030 to .062 mm)
- Wear limit ... ... .006 inch (.15 mm)

Ring end gap (1116 cc):
- Top ring ... ... .0118 to .0177 inch (.30 to .45 mm)
- Middle and bottom rings ... ... .0079 to .0138 inch (.20 to .35 mm)

Ring end gap (1290 cc):
- Top and middle rings ... ... .012 to .018 inch (.30 to .45 mm)
- Bottom ring ... ... .010 to .016 inch (.25 to .40 mm)

Oversize rings available ... ... .0079, .0157 and .0236 inch (.2, .4 and .6 mm)

Piston pins:

Interference fit in small-end (1116 cc) ... .0004 to .0017 inch (.010 to .042 mm)

Clearance fit in small-end (1290 cc) ... .0004 to .0006 inch (.010 to .016 mm)

Clearance fit in piston boss ... ... .0004 to .0007 inch (.010 to .018 mm)

Clearance fit wear limit ... ... .002 inch (.05 mm)

Cylinder head:

Valve stem diameter ... ... .3139 to .3146 inch (7.974 to 7.992 mm)

Stem to guide clearance ... ... .0012 to .0026 inch (.030 to .066 mm)

- Wear limit ... ... .006 inch (.15 mm)
- Valve face angle ... ... 45° 30' ± 5'
- Valve seat angle ... ... 45° ± 5'

Valve timing:

Checked with clearance set to .024 inch (.60 mm) for intake and .026 inch (.65 mm) for exhaust, except Rally models (.020 inch, .50 mm clearance)

All 128 models and 128 3P-1300:
- Intake opens ... ... 12° BTDC
- Intake closes ... ... 52° ABDC
- Exhaust opens ... ... 52° BBDC
- Exhaust closes ... ... 12° ATDC

128 3P-1100:
- Intake opens ... ... 20° BTDC
- Intake closes ... ... 44° ABDC
- Exhaust opens ... ... 60° BBDC
- Exhaust closes ... ... 4° ATDC

128 Rally:
- Intake opens ... ... 24° BTDC
- Intake closes ... ... 68° ABDC
- Exhaust opens ... ... 64° BBDC
- Exhaust closes ... ... 28° ATDC

Valve clearances (cold):

128 models, intake	.012 inch (.30 mm)
exhaust	.016 inch (.40 mm)
128 3P models, intake	.016 inch (.40 mm)
exhaust	.020 inch (.50 mm)
Rally models, intake	.016 inch (.40 mm)
exhaust	.018 inch (.45 mm)

Engine lubrication:

Oil pump	Gear type
Pressure (engine hot)	50 to 70 lb/sq inch (3.5 to 5 kg/sq cm)
Clearance between gears and pump cover ...	.0008 to .0041 inch (.020 to .105 mm)
Clearance between gears and pump walls ...	.0043 to .0071 inch (.110 to .180 mm)

CARBURETTER

Application:

1100	Weber 32 ICEV, 32 ICEV 10, 32 ICEV 14 or Solex DISA 20 or DISA 41
1300	Weber 32 ICEV 13, ICEV 18, Solex 32 DISA 20, DISA 25 or DISA 40
Rally	Weber 32 DMTR or Weber 32 DMTR 20
S, SL Coupé	Weber 32 DMTR 20
3P Berlinetta	Weber 32 DMTR 32

Type:

	32 ICEV	32 ICEV 10	32 ICEV 13
Bore	32	32	32
Venturi...	24	24	24
Auxiliary venturi	4	4	3.5
Main jet	1.25	1.25	1.25
Idling jet	.40	.40	.50
Air correction jet	1.50	1.50	1.50
Idling air jet	1.60	1.60	1.60
Pump jet	.40	.40	.40
Power jet	1.10	1.10	1.10
Power air metering jet	1.00	1.40	1.40
Power mixture orifice	2.00	2.00	2.00

Type:

	32 ICEV 14	32 ICEV 18	32 DISA 20	32 DISA 25	32 DISA 40	32 DISA 41
Bore	32	32	32	32	32	32
Venturi	21	24	24	24	24	21
Auxiliary venturi	3.5	3.5	5	3.4	3.4	3.4
Main jet	1.17	1.22	1.40	1.37	1.35	1.175
Idling jet	.50	1.50	.52	.47	.47	.45
Air correction jet	1.90	.50	1.90	1.70	1.60	1.80
Idling air jet	1.60	1.60	1.00	.60	.60	.60
Pump jet	.40	.40	.45	.50	.50	.50
Power jet	1.10	1.10	.50	.50	1.05	.90
Power air metering jet ...	1.40	1.40	–	–	–	–
Power mixture orifice ...	2.00	2.00	–	–	–	–

Type:

						32 DMTR	
						Primary	*Secondary*
Venturi...	...	...	...	...	...	22	22
Main jet	...	...	...	...	...	1.05	1.15
Idling jet	...	...	...	...	...	.50	.70
Air correction jet	...	...	...	...		1.95	2.00
Idling air jet	...	...	...	...	...	1.00	.70
Pump jet	...	...	...	...	...	.40	—

Type:

					32 DMTR 20	
As 32 DMTR except:						*Primary*	*Secondary*
Main jet	...	...	...	...	...	1.10 (Rally 1.05)	1.15
Air correction jet	...	...	...	...		2.10 (Rally 1.95)	1.90 (Rally 2.00)

Type:

					32 DMTR 32	
As 32 DMTR except:						*Primary*	*Secondary*
Main jet	...	...	...	...	...	1.10	1.10
Air correction jet	...	...	...	...		2.20	1.90

CLUTCH, TRANSMISSION, DIFFERENTIAL

Clutch:

Type	Single plate, dry
Throwout mechanism	Diaphragm spring
Driven plate	With friction linings
Lining O.D.	$7\frac{5}{32}$ inch (181.5 mm)
Lining I.D.	5 inch (127 mm)
Max. runout of driven plate linings	.01 inch (.25 mm)
Clutch pedal free travel, corresponding to a clearance of .079 inch (2 mm) between friction ring and throwout sleeve, abt.	1 inch (25 mm)
Travel of release flange, corresponding to a pressure plate displacement not less than .055 inch (1.4 mm)	.315 inch (8 mm)

Transmission, differential:

Speeds	Four forward and reverse
Synchronizers, spring ring type	1st, 2nd, 3rd and 4th gears

Gear type:

Forward	Constant mesh, helical toothed
Reverse	Straight toothed, with sliding idler gear

Gear ratios:

First...	3.583 : 1
Second	2.235 : 1
Third	1.454 : 1
Fourth	1.042 : 1 (Rally 1.037 : 1)
Reverse	3.714 : 1

Final drive ratio:

To May 1976	4.077 :1 (13/53); Estate 4.417 (12/53)
From May 1976	3.760 :1 (17/64); Estate 4.077 (13/53)

Wheel ratios:

	1st	2nd	3rd	4th	reverse
Gears					
Reduction ratio to 1, Saloon	14.61	9.11	5.93	4.23	15.14
Estate	15.79	9.83	6.39	4.59	16.36

Differential case bearings	2
Bearing type	Taper roller
Bearing pre-load setting	By shims
Side-to-pinion gear backlash adjustment ...	By thrust washers

Power drive to front wheels	By axle shafts connected to differential through 'Tripode' constant-speed joints and to wheels through constant-speed ball joints

Lube oil:

Grade	Fiat ZC90 (SAE.90.EP)
Capacity	3.15 lts, 5.5 pts

FRONT SUSPENSION

Type	Independent wheel. Lower control arms; telescoping knuckle pillars incorporated with hydraulic shock absorbers; coil springs and anti-roll bar

Steering knuckles:

	Saloon/Estate	Sport/3P	Rally
Caster, loaded	2° to 2° 30'		
Caster, unloaded	1° 25' to 1° 55'		
1973 on:			
Caster, loaded	2° to 2° 30'		
Caster, unloaded	1° 10' to 2° 10'	1° 10' to 2° 10'	0° 50' to 1° 50'
Adjustment	By shims set between end stops of sway bar and control arm bushings		

Front wheels:

	Saloon/Estate	Sport/3P	Rally
Camber, loaded	0° 40' to 1° 20'		
Camber, unloaded	1° 20' to 2°		
1973 on:			
Camber loaded	0° 40' to 1° 40'		
Camber, unloaded	1° 10' to 2° 10'	0° 50' to 1° 50'	1° to 2°
Toe-in, loaded	0 ± .039 inch (0 ± 1 mm)		
Toe-in, unloaded	−.197 ± .039 inch (−5 ± 1 mm)		
1973 on:			
Toe-in, loaded	0 to .04 inch (0 to 1 mm)		
Toe-in, unloaded	−.12 to +.04 inch (−3 to +1 mm)	−.06 to +.10 inch (−1.5 to +2.5 mm)	−.10 to +.06 inch (−2.5 to +1.5 mm)
Adjustment	By threaded sleeves in track rods		

Coil springs:

Length under a load of 617± 22 lbs (280± 10 kg)   9.449 inch (240 mm)
Minimum permissible load referred to this length   562 lbs (255 kg)
Coil springs are classified into two categories being marked as follows:
    Yellow daub, springs which develop a length above 9.449 inch (240 mm) under a load of 617 lbs (280 kg) ± 22 lbs (10 kg);
    Green daub, springs which develop a length equal to or less than 9.449 inch (240 mm) in the same conditions.
Spring pairs belonging to the same category should be fitted.

Shock absorbers:

Type	Hydraulic telescopic double acting
Pressure cylinder bore	1.063 inch (27 mm)
Stroke	5.728 inch (145.5 mm)
Fluid quality	Fiat S.A.I.
Fluid capacity	⅖ pints (.225 lt)

*Car loaded: four persons plus 88 lbs (40 kg) luggage.

REAR SUSPENSION

Type	Independent wheel. Lower control arms; telescoping knuckle pillars incorporated with hydraulic shock absorbers; cross semi-elliptic spring and resilient buffers acting on control arms

Rear wheels :

Saloon/Estate

Camber, loaded	–2° 40′ to –3° 20′	
Camber, unloaded	–0° 30′ to +0° 10′	

1973 on :

	Saloon	Estate	Sport/3P	Rally
Camber unloaded	–0° 40′ to +0°20′	+0° 10′ to +1° 10′	–0° 40′ to –1° 40′	0° to –1°

Adjustment	Shims
Toe-in, loaded	.197 ± .079 inch (5 ± 2 mm)
Toe-in, unloaded	.177 ± .079 inch (4.5 ⊥ 2 mm)

1973 on:

	Saloon/Estate	Others
Toe-in, unloaded	+.06 to +.22 inch (+1.5 to +5.5 mm)	+.08 to +.22 inch (+2 to +6 mm)
Adjustment	Shims	

Semi-elliptic spring :

Mounted on control arms and underbody with interposition of rubber pads.

Composition (Saloon)	Two leaves
Camber (under static load)	.630 ± .12 inch (16 ± 3 mm)
Static load for testing	728 lbs (330 kg)
Deflection rate	.678 ± .054 inch/100 lbs (38 ± 3 mm/100 kg)
Composition (Estate)	Three leaves
Camber (under static load)	.511 ± .12 inch (13 ± 3 mm)
Static load	860 lbs (390 kg)
Deflection rate	.569 ± .045 inch/100 lbs (3.18 ± 2.50 mm/100 kg)

Shock absorbers:

Type	Hydraulic telescopic double acting
Pressure cylinder bore	1.063 inch (27 mm)
Stroke (abutting begins)	7.927± .079 inch (202.5± 2 mm)
Fluid quality	Fiat S.A.I.
Fluid capacity	½ pint (0.250 lt)

* Car loaded: four persons plus 88 lbs (40 kg) luggage.

STEERING SYSTEM

Steering gear type	Rack and pinion
Gear ratio:	
Steering wheel turns, lock to lock	3.4
Corresponding rack travel	5.118 inch (130 mm)
Pinion bearings	Ball
Bearing adjustment	By shims set between pinion cover and ballbearing
Adjusting rack to pinion lash	By spring-loaded support and shims set between cover of rack centre pawl and gear housing
Turning circle diameter	33 ft 10 inch (10.30 m)
Track rods	Adjustable

Lock angle :
Outer wheel	...	...	...	...	31 deg. 45'
Inner wheel	...	...	...	...	35 deg.

Steering gear oil :
Grade	...	...	...	...	Fiat W 90/M (SAE.90.EP)
Capacity	...	...	...	...	¼ pint (0.14 lt)

BRAKES

Front:

Type ...	...	...	...	Disc brakes, pedal operated

Brake discs:
Diameter	...	...	...	8.937 inch (227 mm)

Thickness:
Nominal ...	...	...	...	.392 to .400 inch (9.95 to 10.15 mm)
Minimum after refacing ...	...	...		.368 inch (9.35 mm)
Minimum from wear ...	...	...		.354 inch (9 mm)
Max. runout (indicator reading) ...	...	...		.0059 inch (.15 mm)
Brake calipers ...	...	...	...	Floating type, single cylinder
Caliper cylinder bore ...	...	...	...	1.890 inch (48 mm)
Lining clearance adjustment ...	...	...		Automatic

Rear:

Type ...	...	...	...	Drum brakes, pedal operated; self-centring shoes and automatic play take-up
Drum diameter ...	...	...	...	7.2929 to 7.3043 inch (185.24 to 185.53 mm)
Drum refacing: max. oversize allowed on diameter				.0315 inch (.8 mm)
Max. permissible diameter from wear ...	...			7.3554 inch (186.83 mm)

Brake linings:
Length (developed) ...	...	...	...	7.0865 inch (180 mm)
Width ...	...	...	...	1.1811 inch (30 mm)

Thickness:
New ...	...	...	...	.1654 to .1772 inch (4.2 to 4.5 mm)
Minimum permissible ...	...	...		.0591 inch (1.5 mm)
Wheel cylinder bore ...	...	...		¾ inch (19.05 mm)
Master cylinder bore, front and rear circuit ...				¾ inch (19.05 mm)
Hand parking brake ...	...	...	...	Mechanical, on rear wheels
Pressure regulator ...	...	...	...	Affecting rear brakes
Ratio ...	...	...	...	.46:1

Hydraulic fluid, front and rear circuit:
Type ...	...	...	...	Fiat special 'blue label'
Capacity ...	...	...	...	½ pint (.315 lt)

IGNITION SYSTEM

Ignition distributor :

Type	...	...	...	...	S 135B
Static advance	...	...	...	...	10 deg. (1300 cc 5 deg. after 1976)
Centrifugal advance	...	...	...	...	28 deg. ± 2 deg. at 4700 rev/min
Breaker contact pressure	...	...	...		19.4 ± 1.8 oz (550 ± 50 gr)
Contact gap ...	...	...	...	...	.014 to .017 inch (.37 to .43 mm)
Terminal to ground insulation at 500 V dc	...				50 Megohms
Condenser capacity at 50 to 100 Hz ...		...			.22 to .23 microfarad
Opening angle ...	...	...	...	...	35 deg. ± 3 deg.
Closing angle ...	...	...	...	...	55 deg. ± 3 deg.

Ignition coil:						Marelli	Martinetti	Bosch
Type	...	...	...	...	...	BE 200 B	G 52 S	K 12 V
Spark plugs:						*Marelli*	*Champion*	*Bosch*
Type	...	...	...			CW 7 LP	N 9 Y	W 175 T 30
Thread diam. and pitch, metric	...	...	...			M 14 × 1.25	M 14 × 1.25	M 14 × 1.25
Gap	...	...	...			.024 to .028 inch (.6 to .7 mm)	.024 to .028 inch (.6 to .7 mm)	.024 to .028 inch (.6 to .7 mm)

ELECTRICAL SYSTEM

Generator:
Type	...	...	...	...	...	Bosch D90/12/16/3E
Nominal voltage	...	...	...	...		12 volts
Output	...	...	...	...	...	230 W
Cut-in speed	...	...	...	...		1750 rev/min
Direction of rotation	...	...	...	...		Clockwise
Drive ratio	...	...	...	...		1 : 1.86

Alternator:
Type	...	...	...	...	...	Bosch G 1-14V 33 A 27 or Marelli
Output	...	...	...	...	...	38 amps AA108 14V 33A
Drive ratio	...	...	...	...		1 : 2
Cut-in speed	...	...	...	...		1050 ± 50 rev/min

Regulator:
					...	
Type	...	...	...	...	...	Bosch AD 1/14V
Checking speed	...	...	...	...		4000 to 5000 rev/min

Belt type ... ... Ventiflex 1143

Starter motor:
					...	
Type	...	...	...	...	...	Fiat E.84-08/12 Var.1
Output	...	...	...	...	...	.8 kW
Rotation	...	...	...	...	...	Clockwise

CAPACITIES

Fuel tank	...	...	...	...	...	8.3 gallons (38 litres)
Sport Coupé, 3P	...	...	...	...	11 gallons (50 litres)
Cooling system including heater			...	...	11.5 pints (6.6 litres)
Engine sump, refill	...	...	...	...	7.5 pints (4.3 litres)
Gearbox and final drive	...	...	...	...	5.5 pints (3.15 litres)

TORQUE SPECIFICATIONS

	Part No.	Thread (metric)	Material	Torque lb ft	kg m or m da N
Flywheel mounting screw	4160880	M 10 x 1.25	40 Ni Cr Mo 2 Bon R 120 to 135	65	9
Connecting rod bearing cap screw nut	1/25550/20	M 9 x 1	R 80 (Screw R 100)	36	5
Driven sprocket to cam-shaft screw	4190861	M 10 x 1.25	40 Ni Cr Mo 2 R 120 to 135	61	8.5
Cylinder head hold-down screw	4190029	M 12 x 1.25	R 100	69.0	10.0

Cylinder head stud nut ...	1/61015/21	M 12 x 1.25	R 80 Znt (see **Section 1 : 3**) (Stud R 100)		
Cylinder head extension stud nut	1/61008/11	M 8	Nut R 50 Znt (Stud R 80 Znt)	14	2
Main bearing cap screw ...	1/42344/30	M 10 x 1.25	R 100	61	8.5
Fan and water pump drive pulley nut	4179194	M 20 x 1.5	R 50 Znt	101	14
Timing belt stretcher stud nut	1/21647/11	M 10 x 1.25	R 50 Znt (Stud R 100)	33	4.5
Intake and exhaust manifold to cylinder head stud nut	1/61008/11	M 8	Nut R 50 Znt (Stud R 80 Znt)	22	3
Water pump upper bracket stud nut	1/61008/11	M 8	R 50 Znt (Stud R 80 Znt)	18	2.5
Generator lower mounting bracket stud nut	1/21647/11	M 10 x 1.25	R 50 Znt (Stud R 80 Znt)	36	5
Clutch:					
Screw, clutch to flywheel	1/38243/21	M 6	R 80 Znt	11	1.5
Transmission and differential:					
Screw, transmission to engine	1/55411/21	M 12 x 1.25	R 80 Znt	58	8
Nut, transmission to engine	1/61015/11	M 12 x 1.25	R 50 Znt (Stud R 80)	58	8
Screw, ring gear to differential case	4146132	M 8	40 Ni Cr Mo 2 R 120 to 135	36	5
Nut, differential case flange to transmission main case	1/61008/11	M 8	R 50 Znt (Stud R 80)	18	2.5
Screw, front axle shaft coupling sleeve	1/60439/71	M 8	R 120 Cdt	33	4.5
Power plant mountings:					
Nut, power plant mounting pad to body screw, engine end	1/21647/11	M 10 x 1.25	R 50 Znt (Screw R 80 Znt)	25	3.5
Screw, power plant mounting rail to body, transmission end	1/60436/21	M 8	R 80 Znt	18	2.5
Nut, power plant mounting pad bracket to transmission	1/61008/11	M 8	R 50 Znt (Stud R 80)	18	2.5
Screw, power plant anchor rod	1/61365/21	M 8	R 80 Znt	18	2.5
Front suspension:					
Nut, front wheel hub ...	4219934	M 18 x 1.5	C 40 Cdt yellow (Coupl. 20 NCD 2 Cmt)	101	14
Nut, self-locking, front control arm to body ...	1/61044/11	M 8	R 50 Znt (Screw R 80 Znt)	18	2.5

Description	Part No.	Thread	Material/Finish		
Nut, self-locking, steering knuckle ball joint	1/61051/11	M 12 x 1.25	R 50 Znt (Stud 40 Ni Cr Mo 2 R 120 to 135)	25.5	3.5
Nut, front shock absorber upper mounting	4188727	M 10 x 1.25	R 80 Znt	18	2.5
Nut, self-locking, sway bar to control arm	1/25758/11	M 14 x 1.5	R 50 Znt	43	6
Nut, sway bar bracket to body mounting screw ...	2/21647/11	M 10 x 1.25	R 50 Znt (Screw R 50)	22	3
Nut, self-locking, shock absorber to steering knuckle screw	1/25745/21	M 10 x 1.25	R 80 Cdt yellow (Screw R 100)	43	6
Screw, brake caliper assembly to steering knuckle	4164496	M 10 x 1.25	R 80 Fosf	36	5
Rear suspension:					
Nut, leaf spring buffer to rear control arm	1/21647/11	M 10 x 1.25	R 50 Znt (Screw R 50)	22	3
Nut, self-locking, control arm to steering knuckle screw	1/61050/11	M 12 x 1.25	R 50 Znt (Screw R 80)	72	10
Nut, control arm pin to body	1/21647/11	M 10 x 1.25	R 50 Znt (Screw R 80)	36	5
Nut, self-locking, control arm pivot bar bushings ...	1/40488/11	M 12 x 1.25	R 50 Cdt (Bar R 75)	36 / 36	5 / 5
Nut, self-locking, telescoping knuckle pillar to body	1/25745/11	M 10 x 1.25	R 50 Znt	18	2.5
Nut, telescoping knuckle pillar to steering knuckle upper mounting screw ...	1/21647/21	M 10 x 1.25	R 80 Znt (Screw R 100)	58	8
Screw, brake backing plate to steering knuckle ...	1/60432/21	M 8	R 80 Znt	18	2.5
Nut, wheel bearing ...	4219934	M 18 x 1.5	C 40 Rct Cdt (Pivot 38 NCD 6)	101	14
Steering:					
Nut, steering wheel to column	1/07914/11	M 16 x 1.5	R 50 Znt (Col. C 30 Norm)	36	5
Nut, track rod end ball stud	4191151	M 14 x 1	R 50 Znt (Screw R 100)	51	7
Nut, self-locking, ball stud to knuckle arm	1/25756/11	M 10 x 1.25	R 50 Znt (Stud 12 NC 3 Ind)	25	3.5
Screw, steering gear to body	1/61355/21	M 8	R 80 Znt	18	2.5

WIRING DIAGRAMS

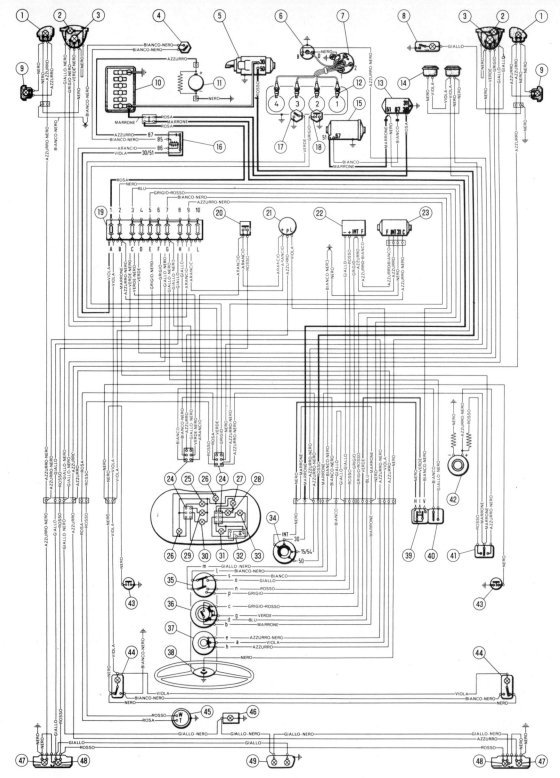

FIG 13:1 Wiring diagram, 128 models with DC generator

Key to Fig 13:1   1 Front direction signal lights   2 Front parking lights   3 High and low beam headlights   4 Thermal switch, controlling cooling fan   5 Starting motor   6 Ignition coil   7 Ignition distributor   8 Engine compartment light, with press switch built-in   9 Side direction signal lights   10 Battery   11 Engine cooling fan motor   12 Spark plugs   13 Generator regulator   14 Horns   15 Generator   16 Cooling fan motor clutch relay   17 Thermal switch for heat indicator   18 Low oil pressure indicator switch   19 Fuses   20 Stop light push switch   21 Direction signal flasher unit   22 Wiper motor timer switch   23 Wiper motor   24 Junction block, wiring harness to instrument cluster   25 Direction signal indicator   26 Instrument cluster lights   27 Heat indicator   28 Low oil pressure indicator   29 Parking light indicator   30 High beam indicator   31 Fuel reserve supply indicator   32 Fuel gauge   33 No-charge indicator   34 Ignition and starting switch, also energizing warning lights circuits   35 Three-position wiper switch   36 Selector switch for outer lights and low beam flashes   37 Direction signal light switch   38 Horn button   39 Outer lighting master switch   40 Instrument cluster light switch   41 Heater fan motor switch, three-position   42 Heater fan motor, two-speed   43 Jam switches on door pillars for courtesy lights   44 Interior lights with built-in switch   45 Fuel gauge tank unit   46 Trunk compartment light   47 Rear direction signal lights   48 Rear parking and stop lights   49 Licence plate lights

Key to cable colours: **Arancio** Orange   **Azzurro** Light blue   **Bianco** White   **Blu** Dark blue   **Giallo** Yellow   **Grigio** Grey   **Marrone** Brown   **Nero** Black   **Rosa** Pink   **Rosso** Red   **Verde** Green   **Viola** Violet   **INT** Switch

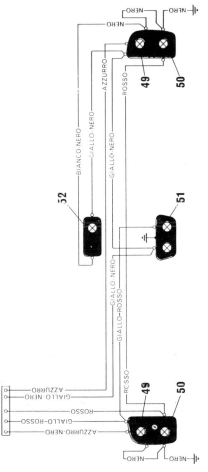

FIG 13:2   128 Estate car variants

Key to Fig 13:2   49 Rear direction indicator lights   50 Rear parking and stop lights   51 Number plate lights   52 Rear quarter lamp, with incorporated switch

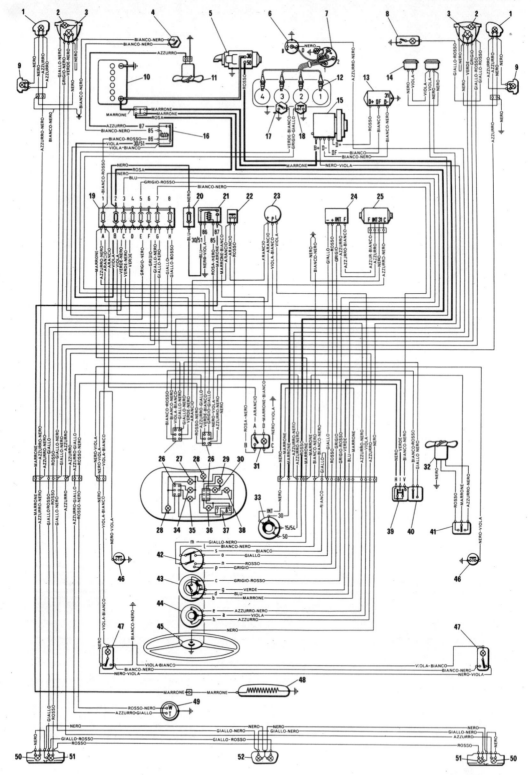

FIG 13:3 Wiring diagram, 128 models with alternator

Key to Fig 13:3 1 Front direction signal lights 2 Front parking lights 3 High and low beam head lights 4 Thermal switch, controlling cooling fan 11 5 Starting motor 6 Ignition coil 7 Ignition distributor 8 Engine compartment light, with press switch built-in 9 Side direction signal lights 10 Battery 11 Engine cooling fan 12 Spark plugs 13 Voltage regulator 14 Horns 15 Alternator 16 Relay, controlling fan 11 17 Thermal sending unit for indicator 29 18 Sending unit for indicator 30 19 Fuses 20 Fuse, for demister 48 (optional) 21 Relay switch for demister 48 (optional) 22 Stop light press switch 23 Direction signal flasher unit 24 Wiper motor timer switch 25 Wiper motor 26 Electric connectors 27 Direction signal repeater (green light) 28 Instrument cluster lights 29 Heater indicator (red light) 30 Low oil pressure indicator (red light) 31 Switch and indicator light for demister 48 (optional) 32 Heater fan motor, two-speed 33 Ignition and starting switch, also energizing warning lights circuits 34 Parking light indicator (green light) 35 High beam indicator (blue light) 36 Low fuel indicator (red light) 37 Fuel gauge 38 No-charge indicator (red light) 39 Outer lighting master switch 40 Instrument cluster light switch 41 Heater fan switch 42 Windshield wiper switch 43 Selector switch for headlights and low beam flashes 44 Direction signal light switch 45 Horn button 46 Courtesy light jam switches on front doors 47 Interior lights, with built-in switch 48 Rear window demister (optional) 49 Fuel gauge tank unit 50 Rear direction signal lights 51 Rear parking and stop lights 52 Licence plate lights

Key to cable colours: **Arancio** Orange **Azzurro** Light blue **Bianco** White **Blu** Dark blue **Giallo** Yellow **Grigio** Grey **Marrone** Brown **Nero** Black **Rosa** Pink **Rosso** Red **Verde** Green **Vicla** Violet **INT** Switch

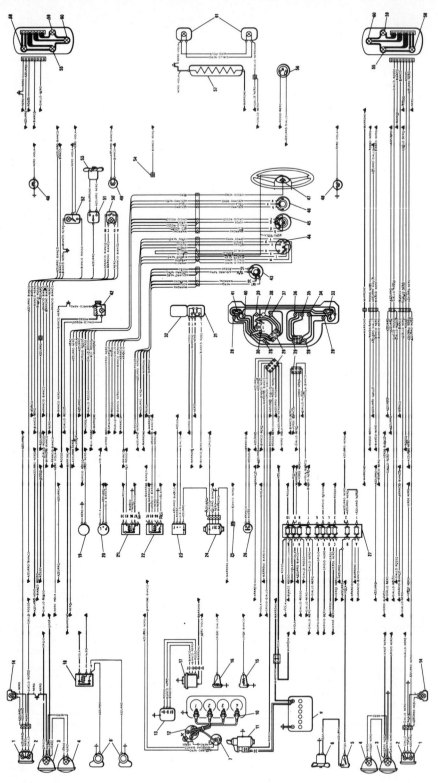

FIG 13:4   Wiring diagram, 128 3P

Key to Fig 13:4   1 Front direction indicators   2 Sidelights   3 Headlights main and dipped beam   4 Headlights main beam   5 Radiator fan switch   6 Radiator fan   7 Ignition coil   8 Horn   9 Battery   10 Spark plugs   11 Starter   12 Distributor   13 Voltage regulator   14 Side repeater indicators   15 Coolant temperature transmitter   16 Oil pressure transmitter   17 Alternator   18 Horn relay   19 Screen washer pump   20 Direction indicator   21 Main beam relay   22 Heated rear window relay   23 Wiper interrupter   24 Wiper motor   25 Brake warning light terminal   26 Stoplight switch   27 Fuses   28 Panel lights   29 Connectors   30 Electronic tachometer   31 Panel light switch   32 Spare switch terminals   33 Coolant temperature gauge   34 Headlamp   35 Direction indicator   36 Sidelight   37 Ignition warning lamp   38 Spare warning light   39 Oil pressure switch   40 Fuel warning light   41 Fuel gauge   42 Cigar lighter   43 Ignition switch   44 Wiper/washer switch   45 Headlamp switch   46 Direction indicator switch   47 Horn switch   48 Door switch   49 Reversing light switch   50 Heated rear window switch   51 Heater fan switch   52 Courtesy light   53 Heater fan motor   54 Brake warning light transmitter   55 Stoplights   56 Fuel gauge transmitter   57 Heated rear window   58 Rear direction indicators   59 Rear lights   60 Reversing lights   61 Number plate light

Key to cable colours: **Arrancio** Amber   **Azzurro** Light blue   **Ben** Dark blue   **Bianco** White   **Giallo** Yellow   **Grigio** Grey   **Maroon** Brown   **Nero** Black   **Rosa** Pink   **Rosso** Red   **Verde** Green   **Viola** Mauve

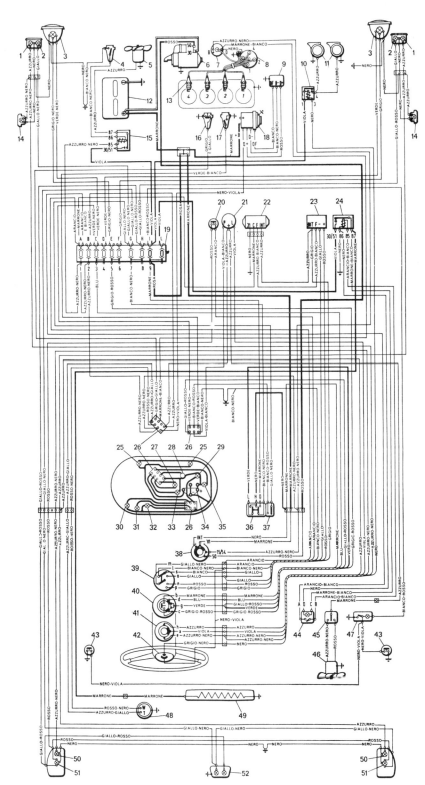

FIG 13:5 Wiring diagram, 128S

Key to Fig 13:5 1 Front direction indicators 2 Front sidelights 3 Main and dipped beam headlights 4 Temperature switch for fan 5 5 Radiator fan 6 Starter 7 Ignition coil 8 Distributor 9 Voltage regulator 10 Horn relay 11 Horns 12 Battery 13 Spark plugs 14 Direction indicator side repeater 15 Relay for fan 5 16 Pressure switch for warning light 35 17 Temperature switch for warning light 28 18 Alternator 19 Fuses 20 Stoplight switch 21 Direction indicator flasher unit 22 Windscreen wiper motor 23 Intermittent windscreen wiper switch 24 Relay for heated rear window 49 (optional) 25 Instrument panel lights 26 Electrical connections on instrument panel 27 Red charge warning light 28 Brake defect warning light (fitted only in those countries in which it is obligatory) 29 Red engine overheating warning light 30 Blue full beam headlight warning light 31 Green direction indicator repeater 32 Green sidelight warning light 33 Red minimum fuel contents warning light 34 Fuel gauge 35 Red oil pressure warning light 36 Road lighting 3-position switch 37 Instrument panel light switch 38 Ignition and starting switch 39 Lever operated 3-position windscreen wiper switch 40 Headlight and daylight flasher switch 41 Direction indicator light operating switch 42 Horn button 43 Door switches 44 Heated rear window switch with built-in indicator light (optional) 45 3-position heater fan switch 46 2-speed heater fan motor 47 Interior-light with built-in switch 48 Fuel contents indicator rheostat 49 Heated rear window (optional) 50 Rear direction indicator lights 51 Tail and stoplights 52 Number plate lights

Key to cable colours: **Arancio** Orange **Bianco** White **Giallo** Yellow **Marrone** Brown **Rosa** Pink **Verde** Green **Azzurro** Light blue **Blu** Dark blue **Grigio** Grey **Nero** Black **Rosso** Red **Viola** Violet

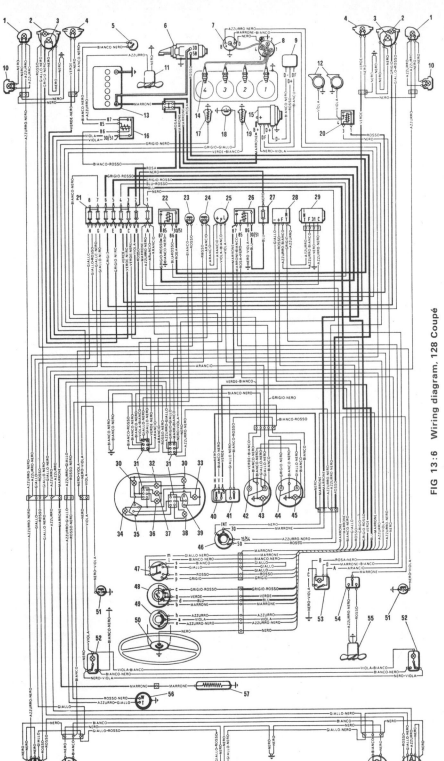

FIG 13:6 Wiring diagram, 128 Coupé

Key to Fig 13:6 1 Front direction indicator light 2 Front sidelights 3 Headlights (halogen vapour) 4 Dipped beam headlight (halogen vapour) 5 Temperature switch for operating motor 11 6 Starter 7 Ignition coil 8 Distributor 9 Voltage regulator 10 Side direction indicator switch 11 Electric fan motor 12 Horns 13 Battery 14 Spark plugs 15 Alternator 16 Relay for operating motor 11 17 Engine oil pressure relay 18 Relay for warning light 33 19 Engine water temperature relay 20 Horn switch 21 System protection fuses 22 Relay for the simultaneous operation of headlights 3 and 4 23 Reversing light switch 24 Stoplight switch 25 Direction indicator flasher unit 26 Relay for unit 57 (optional) 27 Spare fuse for unit 57 (optional) 28 Windscreen wiper intermittent operation system 29 Windscreen wiper motor 30 Instrument panel lights 31 Electrical connections 32 Green direction indicator repeater light 33 Red oil pressure warning light 34 Minimum fuel content red warning light 35 Fuel gauge 36 Blue headlight warning light 37 Green sidelight warning light 38 Red charge warning light 39 Engine electronic tachometer 40 Road lighting switch 41 Instrument panel lighting switch 42 Water temperature indicator 43 Temperature indicator light 44 Oil pressure gauge 45 Pressure gauge light 46 Ignition and starting switch 47 Three position windscreen wiper lever operated switch 48 Road and direction indicator flasher lever 49 Direction indicator light lever 50 Horn button 51 Floor switches 52 Interior light with built in switch 53 Button with built in light for unit 57 (optional) 54 Three position switch for electric fan 55 Heater fan two-speed motor 56 Fuel contents rheostat 57 Rear window demister (optional) 58 Rear direction indicator lights 59 Tail and rear stop lights 60 Reversing lights 61 Number plate lights

Key to cable colours: **Arancio** Orange **Azzurro** Light blue **Blu** Dark blue **Bianco** White **Giallo** Yellow **Marrone** Brown **Rosa** Pink **Verde** Green **Grigio** Grey **Nero** Black **Rosso** Red **Viola** Violet

126

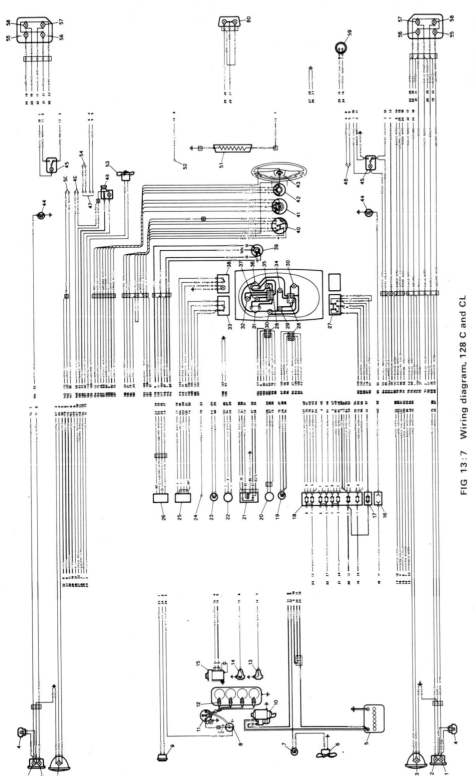

FIG 13:7 Wiring diagram, 128 C and CL

Key to Fig 13:7 1 Front direction indicators 2 Sidelights 3 Headlights main and dipped beam 4 Side repeaters 5 Battery 6 Radiator fan motor 7 Fan switch 8 Ignition coil 9 Horns 10 Starter 11 Distributor 12 Spark plugs 13 Coolant temperature transmitter 14 Oil pressure transmitter 15 Alternator 16 Fuse holder 17 Heated rear window fuse 18 Fuse unit 19 Stoplight switch 20 Electric washer pump 21 Heated rear window relay 22 Direction indicator 23 Reversing light switch 24 Brake warning transmitter 25 Wiper interrupter 26 Wiper motor 27 Panel switch 28 Connectors 29 Direction indicators 30 Panel lights 31 Coolant temperature gauge 32 Ignition warning light 33 Heater fan switch 34 Headlamp warning light 35 Fuel warning light 36 Fuel gauge 37 Oil pressure warning light 38 Heated rear window switch 39 Ignition switch 40 Wiper switch 41 Headlamp switch 42 Indicator switch 43 Horn switch 44 Front door switch 45 Courtesy lights 46 Lefthand speaker leads 47 Radio lead 48 Cigar lighter 49 Radio leads 50 Brake warning light leads 51 Heated rear window 52 Brake warning light switch leads 53 Heater fan motor 54 Righthand speaker leads 55 Rear direction indicators 56 Stoplights 57 Rear lights 58 Reversing lights 59 Fuel gauge transmitter 60 Licence plate lights

Key to cable colours: As for Fig 13:4

NOTES

HINTS ON MAINTENANCE AND OVERHAUL

There are few things more rewarding than the restoration of a vehicle's original peak of efficiency and smooth performance.

The following notes are intended to help the owner to reach that state of perfection. Providing that he possesses the basic manual skills he should have no difficulty in performing most of the operations detailed in this manual. It must be stressed, however, that where recommended in the manual, highly-skilled operations ought to be entrusted to experts, who have the necessary equipment, to carry out the work satisfactorily.

Quality of workmanship:

The hazardous driving conditions on the roads to-day demand that vehicles should be as nearly perfect, mechanically, as possible. It is therefore most important that amateur work be carried out with care, bearing in mind the often inadequate working conditions, and also the inferior tools which may have to be used. It is easy to counsel perfection in all things, and we recognize that it may be setting an impossibly high standard. We do, however, suggest that every care should be taken to ensure that a vehicle is as safe to take on the road as it is humanly possible to make it.

Safe working conditions:

Even though a vehicle may be stationary, it is still potentially dangerous if certain sensible precautions are not taken when working on it while it is supported on jacks or blocks. It is indeed preferable not to use jacks alone, but to supplement them with carefully placed blocks, so that there will be plenty of support if the car rolls off the jacks during a strenuous manoeuvre. Axle stands are an excellent way of providing a rigid base which is not readily disturbed. Piles of bricks are a dangerous substitute. Be careful not to get under heavy loads on lifting tackle, the load could fall. It is preferable not to work alone when lifting an engine, or when working underneath a vehicle which is supported well off the ground. To be trapped, particularly under the vehicle, may have unpleasant results if help is not quickly forthcoming. Make some provision, however humble, to deal with fires. Always disconnect a battery if there is a likelihood of electrical shorts. These may start a fire if there is leaking fuel about. This applies particularly to leads which can carry a heavy current, like those in the starter circuit. While on the subject of electricity, we must also stress the danger of using equipment which is run off the mains and which has no earth or has faulty wiring or connections. So many workshops have damp floors, and electrical shocks are of such a nature that it is sometimes impossible to let go of a live lead or piece of equipment due to the muscular spasms which take place.

Work demanding special care:

This involves the servicing of braking, steering and suspension systems. On the road, failure of the braking system may be disastrous. Make quite sure that there can be no possibility of failure through the bursting of rusty brake pipes or rotten hoses, nor to a sudden loss of pressure due to defective seals or valves.

Problems:

The chief problems which may face an operator are:
1 External dirt.
2 Difficulty in undoing tight fixings
3 Dismantling unfamiliar mechanisms.
4 Deciding in what respect parts are defective.
5 Confusion about the correct order for reassembly.
6 Adjusting running clearances.
7 Road testing.
8 Final tuning.

Practical suggestions to solve the problems:

1 Preliminary cleaning of large parts—engines, transmissions, steering, suspensions, etc.,—should be carried out before removal from the car. Where road dirt and mud alone are present, wash clean with a high-pressure water jet, brushing to remove stubborn adhesions, and allow to drain and dry. Where oil or grease is also present, wash down with a proprietary compound (Gunk, Teepol etc.,) applying with a stiff brush—an old paint brush is suitable—into all crevices. Cover the distributor and ignition coils with a polythene bag and then apply a strong water jet to clear the loosened deposits. Allow to drain and dry. The assemblies will then be sufficiently clean to remove and transfer to the bench for the next stage.

On the bench, further cleaning can be carried out, first wiping the parts as free as possible from grease with old newspaper. Avoid using rag or cotton waste which can leave clogging fibres behind. Any remaining grease can be removed with a brush dipped in paraffin. If necessary, traces of paraffin can be removed by carbon tetrachloride. Avoid using paraffin or petrol in large quantities for cleaning in enclosed areas, such as garages, on account of the high fire risk.

When all exteriors have been cleaned, and not before, dismantling can be commenced. This ensures that dirt will not enter into interiors and orifices revealed by dismantling. In the next phases, where components have to be cleaned, use carbon tetrachloride in preference to petrol and keep the containers covered except when in use. After the components have been cleaned, plug small holes with tapered hard wood plugs cut to size and blank off larger orifices with greaseproof paper and masking tape. Do not use soft wood plugs or matchsticks as they may break.

2 It is not advisable to hammer on the end of a screw thread, but if it must be done, first screw on a nut to protect the thread, and use a lead hammer. This applies particularly to the removal of tapered cotters. Nuts and bolts seem to 'grow' together, especially in exhaust systems. If penetrating oil does not work, try the judicious application of heat, but be careful of starting a fire. Asbestos sheet or cloth is useful to isolate heat.

Tight bushes or pieces of tail-pipe rusted into a silencer can be removed by splitting them with an open-ended hacksaw. Tight screws can sometimes be started by a tap from a hammer on the end of a suitable screwdriver. Many tight fittings will yield to the judicious use of a hammer, but it must be a soft-faced hammer if damage is to be avoided, use a heavy block on the opposite side to absorb shock. Any parts of the steering system which have been damaged should be renewed, as attempts to repair them may lead to cracking and subsequent failure, and steering ball joints should be disconnected using a recommended tool to prevent damage.

3 If often happens that an owner is baffled when trying to dismantle an unfamiliar piece of equipment. So many modern devices are pressed together or assembled by spinning-over flanges, that they must be sawn apart. The intention is that the whole assembly must be renewed. However, parts which appear to be in one piece to the naked eye, may reveal close-fitting joint lines when inspected with a magnifying glass, and, this may provide the necessary clue to dismantling. Left-handed screw threads are used where rotational forces would tend to unscrew a right handed screw thread.

Be very careful when dismantling mechanisms which may come apart suddenly. Work in an enclosed space where the parts will be contained, and drape a piece of cloth over the device if springs are likely to fly in all directions. Mark everything which might be reassembled in the wrong position, scratched symbols may be used on unstressed parts, or a sequence of tiny dots from a centre punch can be useful. Stressed parts should never be scratched or centre-popped as this may lead to cracking under working conditions. Store parts which look alike in the correct order for reassembly. Never rely upon memory to assist in the assembly of complicated mechanisms, especially when they will be dismantled for a long time, but make notes, and drawings to supplement the diagrams in the manual, and put labels on detached wires. Rust stains may indicate unlubricated wear. This can sometimes be seen round the outside edge of a bearing cup in a universal joint. Look for bright rubbing marks on parts which normally should not make heavy contact. These might prove that something is bent or running out of truth. For example, there might be bright marks on one side of a piston, at the top near the ring grooves, and others at the bottom of the skirt on the other side. This could well be the clue to a bent connecting rod. Suspected cracks can be proved by heating the component in a light oil to approximately 100°C, removing, drying off, and dusting with french chalk, if a crack is present the oil retained in the crack will stain the french chalk.

4 In determining wear, and the degree, against the permissible limits set in the manual, accurate measurement can only be achieved by the use of a micrometer. In many cases, the wear is given to the fourth place of decimals; that is in ten-thousandths of an inch. This can be read by the vernier scale on the barrel of a good micrometer. Bore diameters are more difficult to determine. If, however, the matching shaft is accurately measured, the degree of play in the bore can be felt as a guide to its suitability. In other cases, the shank of a twist drill of known diameter is a handy check.

Many methods have been devised for determining the clearance between bearing surfaces. To-day the best and simplest is by the use of Plastigage, obtainable from most garages. A thin plastic thread is laid between the two surfaces and the bearing is tightened, flattening the thread. On removal, the width of the thread is compared with a scale supplied with the thread and the clearance is read off directly. Sometimes joint faces leak persistently, even after gasket renewal. The fault will then be traceable to distortion, dirt or burrs. Studs which are screwed into soft metal frequently raise burrs at the point of entry. A quick cure for this is to chamfer the edge of the hole in the part which fits over the stud.

5 **Always check a replacement part with the original one before it is fitted.**

If parts are not marked, and the order for reassembly is not known, a little detective work will help. Look for marks which are due to wear to see if they can be mated. Joint faces may not be identical due to manufacturing errors, and parts which overlap may be stained, giving a clue to the correct position. Most fixings leave identifying marks especially if they were painted over on assembly. It is then easier to decide whether a nut, for instance, has a plain, a spring, or a shakeproof washer under it. All running surfaces become 'bedded' together after long spells of work and tiny imperfections on one part will be found to have left corresponding marks on the other. This is particularly true of shafts and bearings and even a score on a cylinder wall will show on the piston.

6 Checking end float or rocker clearances by feeler gauge may not always give accurate results because of wear. For instance, the rocker tip which bears on a valve stem may be deeply pitted, in which case the feeler will simply be bridging a depression. Thrust washers may also wear depressions in opposing faces to make accurate measurement difficult. End float is then easier to check by using a dial gauge. It is common practice to adjust end play in bearing assemblies, like front hubs with taper rollers, by doing up the axle nut until the hub becomes stiff to turn and then backing it off a little. Do not use this method with ballbearing hubs as the assembly is often preloaded by tightening the axle nut to its fullest extent. If the splitpin hole will not line up, file the base of the nut a little.

Steering assemblies often wear in the straight-ahead position. If any part is adjusted, make sure that it remains free when moved from lock to lock. Do not be surprised if an assembly like a steering gearbox, which is known to be carefully adjusted outside the car, becomes stiff when it is bolted in place. This will be due to distortion of the case by the pull of the mounting bolts, particularly if the mounting points are not all touching together. This problem may be met in other equipment and is cured by careful attention to the alignment of mounting points.

When a spanner is stamped with a size and A/F it means that the dimension is the width between the jaws and has no connection with ANF, which is the designation for the American National Fine thread. Coarse threads like Whitworth are rarely used on cars to-day except for studs which screw into soft aluminium or cast iron. For this reason it might be found that the top end of a cylinder head stud has a fine thread and the lower end a coarse thread to screw into the cylinder block. If the car has mainly UNF threads then it is likely that any coarse threads will be UNC, which are not the same as Whitworth. Small sizes have the same number of threads in Whitworth and UNC, but in the $\frac{1}{2}$ inch size for example, there are twelve threads to the inch in the former and thirteen in the latter.

7 After a major overhaul, particularly if a great deal of work has been done on the braking, steering and suspension systems, it is advisable to approach the problem of testing with care. If the braking system has been overhauled, apply heavy pressure to the brake pedal and get a second operator to check every possible source of leakage. The brakes may work extremely well, but a leak could cause complete failure after a few miles.

Do not fit the hub caps until every wheel nut has been checked for tightness, and make sure the tyre pressures are correct. Check the levels of coolant, lubricants and hydraulic fluids. Being satisfied that all is well, take the car on the road and test the brakes at once. Check the steering and the action of the handbrake. Do all this at moderate speeds on quiet roads, and make sure there is no other vehicle behind you when you try a rapid stop.

Finally, remember that many parts settle down after a time, so check for tightness of all fixings after the car has been on the road for a hundred miles or so.

8 It is useless to tune an engine which has not reached its normal running temperature. In the same way, the tune of an engine which is stiff after a rebore will be different when the engine is again running free. Remember too, that rocker clearances on pushrod operated valve gear will change when the cylinder head nuts are tightened after an initial period of running with a new head gasket.

Trouble may not always be due to what seems the obvious cause. Ignition, carburation and mechanical condition are interdependent and spitting back through the carburetter, which might be attributed to a weak mixture, can be caused by a sticking inlet valve.

For one final hint on tuning, never adjust more than one thing at a time or it will be impossible to tell which adjustment produced the desired result.

NOTES

GLOSSARY OF TERMS

Allen key   Cranked wrench of hexagonal section for use with socket head screws.

Alternator   Electrical generator producing alternating current. Rectified to direct current for battery charging.

Ambient temperature   Surrounding atmospheric temperature.

Annulus   Used in engineering to indicate the outer ring gear of an epicyclic gear train.

Armature   The shaft carrying the windings, which rotates in the magnetic field of a generator or starter motor. That part of a solenoid or relay which is activated by the magnetic field.

Axial   In line with, or pertaining to, an axis.

Backlash   Play in meshing gears.

Balance lever   A bar where force applied at the centre is equally divided between connections at the ends.

Banjo axle   Axle casing with large diameter housing for the crownwheel and differential.

Bendix pinion   A self-engaging and self-disengaging drive on a starter motor shaft.

Bevel pinion   A conical shaped gearwheel, designed to mesh with a similar gear with an axis usually at 90 deg. to its own.

bhp   Brake horse power, measured on a dynamometer.

bmep   Brake mean effective pressure. Average pressure on a piston during the working stroke.

Brake cylinder   Cylinder with hydraulically operated piston(s) acting on brake shoes or pad(s).

Brake regulator   Control valve fitted in hydraulic braking system which limits brake pressure to rear brakes during heavy braking to prevent rear wheel locking.

Camber   Angle at which a wheel is tilted from the vertical.

Capacitor   Modern term for an electrical condenser. Part of distributor assembly, connected across contact breaker points, acts as an interference suppressor.

Castellated   Top face of a nut, slotted across the flats, to take a locking splitpin.

Castor   Angle at which the kingpin or swivel pin is tilted when viewed from the side.

cc   Cubic centimetres. Engine capacity is arrived at by multiplying the area of the bore in sq cm by the stroke in cm by the number of cylinders.

Clevis   U-shaped forked connector used with a clevis pin, usually at handbrake connections.

Collet   A type of collar, usually split and located in a groove in a shaft, and held in place by a retainer. The arrangement used to retain the spring(s) on a valve stem in most cases.

Commutator   Rotating segmented current distributor between armature windings and brushes in generator or motor.

Compression ratio   The ratio, or quantitative relation, of the total volume (piston at bottom of stroke) to the unswept volume (piston at top of stroke) in an engine cylinder.

Condenser   See capacitor.

Core plug   Plug for blanking off a manufacturing hole in a casting.

Crownwheel   Large bevel gear in rear axle, driven by a bevel pinion attached to the propeller shaft. Sometimes called a 'ring gear'.

'C'-spanner   Like a 'C' with a handle. For use on screwed collars without flats, but with slots or holes.

Damper   Modern term for shock-absorber, used in vehicle suspension systems to damp out spring oscillations.

Depression   The lowering of atmospheric pressure as in the inlet manifold and carburetter.

Dowel   Close tolerance pin, peg, tube, or bolt, which accurately locates mating parts.

Drag link   Rod connecting steering box drop arm (pitman arm) to nearest front wheel steering arm in certain types of steering systems.

Dry liner   Thinwall tube pressed into cylinder bore

Dry sump   Lubrication system where all oil is scavenged from the sump, and returned to a separate tank.

Dynamo   See Generator.

Electrode   Terminal, part of an electrical component, such as the points or 'Electrodes' of a sparking plug.

Electrolyte   In lead-acid car batteries a solution of sulphuric acid and distilled water.

End float   The axial movement between associated parts, end play.

EP   Extreme pressure. In lubricants, special grades for heavily loaded bearing surfaces, such as gear teeth in a gearbox, or crownwheel and pinion in a rear axle.

Fade	Of brakes. Reduced efficiency due to overheating.	**Journals**	Those parts of a shaft that are in contact with the bearings.
Field coils	Windings on the polepieces of motors and generators.	**Kingpin**	The main vertical pin which carries the front wheel spindle, and permits steering movement. May be called 'steering pin' or 'swivel pin'.
Fillets	Narrow finishing strips usually applied to interior bodywork.		
First motion shaft	Input shaft from clutch to gearbox.	**Layshaft**	The shaft which carries the laygear in the gearbox. The laygear is driven by the first motion shaft and drives the third motion shaft according to the gear selected. Sometimes called the 'countershaft' or 'second motion shaft.'
Fullflow filter	Filters in which all the oil is pumped to the engine. If the element becomes clogged, a bypass valve operates to pass unfiltered oil to the engine.		
FWD	Front wheel drive.	**lb ft**	A measure of twist or torque. A pull of 10 lb at a radius of 1 ft is a torque of 10 lb ft.
Gear pump	Two meshing gears in a close fitting casing. Oil is carried from the inlet round the outside of both gears in the spaces between the gear teeth and casing to the outlet, the meshing gear teeth prevent oil passing back to the inlet, and the oil is forced through the outlet port.		
		lb/sq in	Pounds per square inch.
		Little-end	The small, or piston end of a connecting rod. Sometimes called the 'small-end'.
		LT	Low Tension. The current output from the battery.
Generator	Modern term for 'Dynamo'. When rotated produces electrical current.	**Mandrel**	Accurately manufactured bar or rod used for test or centring purposes.
Grommet	A ring of protective or sealing material. Can be used to protect pipes or leads passing through bulkheads.	**Manifold**	A pipe, duct, or chamber, with several branches.
		Needle rollers	Bearing rollers with a length many times their diameter.
Grubscrew	Fully threaded headless screw with screwdriver slot. Used for locking, or alignment purposes.		
		Oil bath	Reservoir which lubricates parts by immersion. In air filters, a separate oil supply for wetting a wire mesh element to hold the dust.
Gudgeon pin	Shaft which connects a piston to its connecting rod. Sometimes called 'wrist pin', or 'piston pin'.		
Halfshaft	One of a pair transmitting drive from the differential.	**Oil wetted**	In air filters, a wire mesh element lightly oiled to trap and hold airborne dust.
Helical	In spiral form. The teeth of helical gears are cut at a spiral angle to the side faces of the gearwheel.	**Overlap**	Period during which inlet and exhaust valves are open together.
Hot spot	Hot area that assists vapourisation of fuel on its way to cylinders. Often provided by close contact between inlet and exhaust manifolds.	**Panhard rod**	Bar connected between fixed point on chassis and another on axle to control sideways movement.
		Pawl	Pivoted catch which engages in the teeth of a ratchet to permit movement in one direction only.
HT	High Tension. Applied to electrical current produced by the ignition coil for the sparking plugs.		
		Peg spanner	Tool with pegs, or pins, to engage in holes or slots in the part to be turned.
Hydrometer	A device for checking specific gravity of liquids. Used to check specific gravity of electrolyte.	**Pendant pedals**	Pedals with levers that are pivoted at the top end.
Hypoid bevel gears	A form of bevel gear used in the rear axle drive gears. The bevel pinion meshes below the centre line of the crownwheel, giving a lower propeller shaft line.	**Phillips screwdriver**	A cross-point screwdriver for use with the cross-slotted heads of Phillips screws.
		Pinion	A small gear, usually in relation to another gear.
Idler	A device for passing on movement. A free running gear between driving and driven gears. A lever transmitting track rod movement to a side rod in steering gear.	**Piston-type damper**	Shock absorber in which damping is controlled by a piston working in a closed oil-filled cylinder.
		Preloading	Preset static pressure on ball or roller bearings not due to working loads.
Impeller	A centrifugal pumping element. Used in water pumps to stimulate flow.	**Radial**	Radiating from a centre, like the spokes of a wheel.

Radius rod	Pivoted arm confining movement of a part to an arc of fixed radius.
Ratchet	Toothed wheel or rack which can move in one direction only, movement in the other being prevented by a pawl.
Ring gear	A gear tooth ring attached to outer periphery of flywheel. Starter pinion engages with it during starting.
Runout	Amount by which rotating part is out of true.
Semi-floating axle	Outer end of rear axle halfshaft is carried on bearing inside axle casing. Wheel hub is secured to end of shaft.
Servo	A hydraulic or pneumatic system for assisting, or, augmenting a physical effort. See 'Vacuum Servo'.
Setscrew	One which is threaded for the full length of the shank.
Shackle	A coupling link, used in the form of two parallel pins connected by side plates to secure the end of the master suspension spring and absorb the effects of deflection.
Shell bearing	Thinwalled steel shell lined with anti-friction metal. Usually semi-circular and used in pairs for main and big-end bearings.
Shock absorber	See 'Damper'.
Silentbloc	Rubber bush bonded to inner and outer metal sleeves.
Socket-head screw	Screw with hexagonal socket for an Allen key.
Solenoid	A coil of wire creating a magnetic field when electric current passes through it. Used with a soft iron core to operate contacts or a mechanical device.
Spur gear	A gear with teeth cut axially across the periphery
Stub axle	Short axle fixed at one end only.
Tachometer	An instrument for accurate measurement of rotating speed. Usually indicates in revolutions per minute.

TDC	Top Dead Centre. The highest point reached by a piston in a cylinder, with the crank and connecting rod in line.
Thermostat	Automatic device for regulating temperature. Used in vehicle coolant systems to open a valve which restricts circulation at low temperature.
Third motion shaft	Output shaft of gearbox.
Threequarter floating axle	Outer end of rear axle halfshaft flanged and bolted to wheel hub, which runs on bearing mounted on outside of axle casing. Vehicle weight is not carried by the axle shaft.
Thrust bearing or washer	Used to reduce friction in rotating parts subject to axial loads.
Torque	Turning or twisting effort. See 'lb ft'.
Track rod	The bar(s) across the vehicle which connect the steering arms and maintain the front wheels in their correct alignment.
UJ	Universal joint. A coupling between shafts which permits angular movement.
UNF	Unified National Fine screw thread.
Vacuum servo	Device used in brake system, using difference between atmospheric pressure and inlet manifold depression to operate a piston which acts to augment brake pressure as required. See 'Servo'.
Venturi	A restriction or 'choke' in a tube, as in a carburetter, used to increase velocity to obtain a reduction in pressure.
Vernier	A sliding scale for obtaining fractional readings of the graduations of an adjacent scale.
Welch plug	A domed thin metal disc which is partially flattened to lock in a recess. Used to plug core holes in castings.
Wet liner	Removable cylinder barrel, sealed against coolant leakage, where the coolant is in direct contact with the outer surface.
Wet sump	A reservoir attached to the crankcase to hold the lubricating oil.

NOTES

INDEX